SAD BOY A

M

All rights reserved; no part of this book may be reproduced by any means without the publisher's permission.

ISBN: 978-1-913642-53-2

The author has asserted their right to be identified as the author of this Work in accordance with the Copyright, Designs and Patents Act 1988

Book designed by Aaron Kent

Edited by Aaron Kent

Broken Sleep Books (2021), Talgarreg, Wales

Contents

Foreword 7

Prologue 13
Towards the Genealogy of a Sad Boy Aesthetics
The aesthetics of the desert – The death drive of capitalist hyperrealism – Death-obsessed lotharios – Trash stars and made-up worlds – ＴＲＡＳＨ 新 ドラゴン *- Liminality, hauntology, depression and its mirrors – Terminal melancholy*

The Way I See Things 29
From Lil Peep to the Hyperreal
Star shopping – Save That Shit – Crybaby – Right Here – Hellboy – Haunt U – Teen Romance – Your Favorite Dress – Yesterday – Beamerboy – Lil Jeep – Life Is Beautiful – About U – Ghost boy – Big City Blues – Nineteen – Me And You – Falling Down – 16 Lines – Awful Things – Witchblades – The Brightside – i crash, u crash – Driveway – The Way I See Things - Benz Truck (гелик) – praying to the sky – Give U The Moon – Ghost Girl – U Said – Runaway – Gym Class – Beat It

Connective Analysis 69
Wittgenstein's Aesthetics and Baudrillard's Aestheticization
Veins & Joji's 'Ballads 1' – Five Degrees of liminal spaces – 4 GOLD CHAINS & promiscuous superficiality – Cobain: images & identities – Nothing To U & occultures – From White Wine to Yukio Mishima – OMFG & the xerox – Lie To Me & Bladee's 'Red Light' –Falling 4 Me: From Saetia to 'OK Computer'

Epilogue 95
Dreams & Disappearances
"Everything miraculous has disappeared" – Terminal futility – Kubrick and Aster as nihilists – The most revealing philosophical text of the twenty-first century could be a Socratic dialogue with Belle Delphine

Selected Notes 103

For Wendy
<3_<3

SAD BOY AESTHETICS

Alex Mazey

(つ◕‿◕)つ

'…other boys be boring.'

Yung Lean, Pikachu

FOREWORD

Ken Hollings

'What does it mean to us today to live philosophically, to be wise?' Nietzsche asks in one of his late notebooks. 'Is it not almost a way of *extricating* oneself cleverly from an ugly game? A kind of flight?' Time and again I catch myself circling back to these questions, especially when thinking about aesthetics. What makes the game so ugly – and will our wits alone be enough to evade it? Rules, after all, are made to be broken or, to be more precise, *reinterpreted*. 'Culture is created through the xeroxing of this radical other,' Alex Mazey writes in *Sad Boy Aesthetics*, reflecting specifically upon the 'amalgamation of tiny insignificances' that lends such an aura of authenticity to our attempts at extrication from the ugly game within which we have managed so carefully to trap ourselves. And what form will this extrication finally take? Intoxication? Bodies and pleasures? Mysticism? Excess? Or can it perhaps be another type of aestheticism altogether? 'In many ways,' Mazey observes, 'a copy is reproduced only through a series of minor absences.' Are we therefore entering a period when each of these absences is now seen entirely in terms of flight? Copies, *Sad Boy Aesthetics* successfully argues, 'create entirely new forms.'

In terms of extrication or flight, these entirely new forms occupy entirely new spaces – which is also to say that they fracture and fragment them. And it is precisely for this reason that Mazey's approach to his subject deserves our attention. Twenty years ago, I started my first book *Destroy All Monsters* with a xeroxed version of a standard sequence in which a child savant's consciousness plunges into a network of fibre-optic cables before getting caught in the digital slipstream of a weapons system operating in the Persian Gulf. 'Something's wrong here,' the child tells himself. 'This isn't MTV.' Then he disappears into an endless black space that slices itself up into sudden panic-filled barrages of TV imagery. Reading *Sad Boy Aesthetics* for the first time put me in mind of that experience. The predictive uniformity of the network, operating as it does in real time, produces an endless fragmentation of experience – and it is in this endless fragmentation of experience that Mazey submerges his reader. The rappers and producers that he discusses exist here as an essential pretext: an open point of immersion. Mazey offers them to us as a succession of entries: temporary spaces – scattered fragments of rhymes, scenarios made up of fleeting details. Nothing is whole. None of the pieces connect. They flicker and then split even further apart.

Under Mazey's restless gaze, such fractures become continuities. His analysis pulls us in deeper. Our experience of this depth, however, should not be mistaken for some new level of wholeness or order. What we are presented with instead is an uneven crosshatching of references, associations and asides. Ridges, lumps and gullies open up everywhere. The text breaks out like an adolescent's skin; and for once we get to see what's happening *above* the surface.

*

It is entirely possible that Nietzsche was thinking about music when he remarked that intellectual development is accompanied by feelings of disgust – perhaps also a sense of betrayal. 'Even in death, Lil Peep reveals something,' Mazey writes – '*especially* in death' is perhaps the inevitable response. 'It is only at the very end of Yukio Mishima's *The Temple of the Golden Pavilion*, for example,' Mazey points out, 'where the protagonist considers the profound beauty of his nihilism, not as a source of mere and mindless destruction, but as the staging force for life's sublimity: an aesthetics of perfect ephemerality.' Music writing lends itself to casual hyperbole, as if the music itself can only exist as a set of superlatives. Too often the writer seems to imply that their entire being is somehow located within that music – but if that should turn out to be the case, what kind of 'being' is it? 'For in music men let themselves go, in belief that when they are concealed in music no one is *capable* of seeing them,' Nietzsche observes parenthetically in *Daybreak* – as if it were too shameful even for a music lover like him to admit to such a thing in the main body of his text. Death will always reveal *something*. And here come those feelings of disgust again…

*

Sad Boy Aesthetics shares with its reader the casual nihilism of a party that never wants to be over, even though it really should have ended a long time ago. Nausea and vertigo become new forms of ecstasy. The glossy surfaces of this world are alive with distorting scratches and reflections.

There is in Mazey's exploration of this hedonistic despair an equally desperate desire for it not to stop. It's the fragments, details and fractures that will save us – precisely because they are fragments, details and fractures. Every aspect, however small, becomes significant in Mazey's text; hotel rooms and magazine articles, films and videogames, quotations and references tumble and collapse into one another as we read. Personal details add further fractures to its already uneven surface. What's important here is the hyperactive intensity of the gaze taking it all in, catching the ephemeral as it falls. There is a numb clarity to the sadness with which each detail has been captured. Music writing would benefit greatly from an extended indifference to its subject from the writer. It takes a certain amount of skill to listen while maintaining the necessary lack of engagement. 'At a hotel in Liverpool, I once made a Bloody Mary at the "Bloody Mary Self-Service Bar" located beside a pile of all-butter croissants,' Mazey recalls, 'not because this had anything to do with any normal morning routine, but simply because the option was available to me.' Is it possible that music is now something to be resisted? Having positioned itself as perhaps the *only* available option, it has subsequently become the hiding place for a whole ragbag assemblage of drives, anxieties and conflicts to conceal themselves. Like the party that never wants to be over, music has transformed itself into an endless distraction within which we are forever free to hide ourselves from ourselves. There is, for example, a strange and alienating poetry to discovering my own words being read so closely and quoted so seriously – especially when they also happen to appear next to an anecdote about an early model flip phone. *Hey*, I told myself, *I used to have the same model too*. Maybe you did too. I can still feel the weight of it resting in the palm of my hand.

Ken Hollings
London, March 2021

PROLOGUE

Towards the Genealogy of a Sad Boy Aesthetics

Sad Boy Aesthetics

One lonely summer, years after they'd electrocuted the Rosenbergs, and my consciousness had been born unfairly into existence (very edgy), a boy was writing his first ever shitpost; a creepypasta[1] about the video game 'Stardew Valley'[2] – I'll spare you the details.

At the beginning of a 1981 philosophical treatise, 'Simulacra and Simulations'[3], Jean Baudrillard writes: 'The simulacrum is never that which conceals the truth--it is the truth which conceals that there is none. The simulacrum is true.' In a meme once observed, late at night, a mysterious non-entity that may or may not exist had replaced the word 'simulacrum' with the term 'shitpost'. 'The shitpost is never that which conceals the truth--it is the truth which conceals that there is none...'

According to the Wiktionary definition: 'shitpost (plural shitposts) (Internet, slang, vulgar, derogatory) A worthless post on a messageboard, newsgroup, or other online discussion platform.' The interchangeability of these terms, simulacrum and shitpost, refers to a coalescence in meaning, I think. That a shitpost, in many ways, doesn't conceal the truth regarding a regular, non-shitpost, but rather conceals the fact that all posts are shitposts.

In many ways, all books are very longwinded shitposts too; especially a book on the genealogy of sad boy aesthetics, which will explore, in more ways than one, the complex aesthetics of Gustav Åhr – better known as Lil Peep – an American rapper, singer, songwriter and model who lived for a short twenty-one years, between November 1, 1996 and November 15, 2017.

Lil Peep 'began making music in his bedroom,' writes David Peisner of 'Rolling Stones Magazine'[4], 'using a MacBook outfitted with GarageBand and a microphone he bought at Guitar Center.' Despite the buzz of an online following that emerged in the earlier years of his SoundCloud success, Gus ended up on the trash heaps of Skid Row, staying in a crowded loft; a dream factory of rappers and producers out to make it big in LA. This was long before his $6,000-a-month stipend provided by First Access Entertainment.

On Skid Row 'he connected with Lil Tracy, Fish Narc and Coldhart,' Peisner continues 'all members of the emo-rap collective Gothboiclique (GBC).' I would be introduced to the conception of such a collective a few months after my foray into creepypasta, when I would first listen to the track 'benz truck (гелик)', and hear the computerised, virtual voice of a feminine entity call out the name, eerily so, 'Gothboiclique'.

'SoundCloud rap is only a few years old,' Peisner concludes, beginning the culmination of an interview with Liza Womack, Gus's mother and producer of the Lil Peep documentary, 'Everybody's Everything'[5]. 'But the careers of three of its most prominent stars — XXXTentacion, Tekashi 6ix9ine and Peep — have ended disastrously.'

It would be easy to write another book about disaster, but this book isn't about disaster since disaster would suggest something has changed in a landscape of the real – rather than diminished. Lil Peep's lifework embodies a mode of disappearance, which makes the aesthetics presented in his lyrics and creative output worthy of an interrogation.

Even in death, Lil Peep reveals something.

'Look,' Womack tells 'Rolling Stones Magazine', 'We think American capitalism is a horrible thing.'

It is no coincidence that Gustav Åhr passed, aged twenty-one, in close proximity to the Sonoran Desert, which embodies, I think, the desert of America itself. This book is a shitpost concerned only with the aesthetics of that Baudrillardian desert from which we will all be commanded to live; an aesthetics of the melancholy.

'We will live in this world,' Baudrillard writes, 'which for us has all the disquieting strangeness of the desert and of the simulacrum, with all the veracity of living phantoms, of wandering and simulating animals that capital, that the death of capital has made of us—because the desert of cities is equal to the desert of sand—the jungle of signs is equal to that of the forests—the vertigo of simulacra is equal to that of nature—only the vertiginous seduction of a dying system remains, in which work buries work, in which value buries value—leaving a virgin, sacred space without pathways, continuous as Bataille wished it, where only the wind lifts the sand, where only the wind watches over the sand.'

(つ◉⌣◉)つ

'By now, very little a few haunting refrains lingering at the back of your mind separates you from the desert of the real.' On page sixty-two of 'Ghosts of my Life'[6], Mark Fisher

– Sad Boy Aesthetics –

referred to 'The male lust for death' prevalent within the surface operations of rock music, having existed long before Ian Curtis intoned his trans-melancholic considerations onto the iconography of a loaded gun.

Fisher was careful to give a genre-specific account on the signs and associations of the death drive as occurring within the pernicious surface-dwelling of rock music, smuggled into the genre by way of 'libidinous pretexts'. Over one-hundred pages later, it seems Fisher projected a similar theory onto the more contemporary manifestations of Drake and Kanye West, who were both 'morbidly fixated on exploring the miserable hollowness at the core of super-affluent hedonism' from which Fisher suggests, albeit sub-textually, I claim, that the consumerist death drive of capitalist realism exists, perhaps, at a pancultural altitude.

Prior to this analysis of mainstream hip-hop, Mark Fisher wrote that 'A secret sadness lurks behind the 21st century's forced smile.' An analysis that seems to run parallel to the Baudrillardian analysis of contemporary fascinations – the smile of Tom Cruise, a given example, existing only as a means of simulation.

'Smile and others will smile back.' Baudrillard writes, 'Smile to show how transparent, how candid you are. Smile if you have nothing to say. Most of all, do not hide the fact you have nothing to say nor your total indifference to others. Let this emptiness, this profound indifference shine out spontaneously in your smile.'

In the cybography of Lil Peep, one of the natural predecessors of hip-hop's 'registered melancholy', the 21st century's forced smile had been dropped to reveal a sadness that was no longer secret but could now exist at the level of collective disclosure. Alternatively, Mark Fisher's analysis of rock music's death drive symbolism could adequately explain why Lil Peep's earliest music, posted to SoundCloud, as previously mentioned, was tagged as '#Alternative Rock', a situation that left many music journalists characteristically disorientated at the time.

The difficulty with Lil Peep's categorisation and analysis can be located in how Gustav Åhr was an artist who was dead serious in a time when irony, in the phrasing of David Foster Wallace, 'tyrannises us' becoming 'the song of a bird that has come to love its cage.'[7] In Lil Peep's mallgoth sincerity,

'I wanna die too / we all wanna die too', the ontologies of a suicidal culture become accelerated, no longer concealed, but made real. Suicide, according to Fisher, had 'the power to transfigure life, with all its quotidian mess, its conflicts, its ambivalences, its disappointments, its unfinished business, its waste and fever and heat – into a cold myth...' It could be said that the seriousness of Lil Peep's confessionalism, in hindsight, only became solidified in his death, since 'Suicide was a guarantee of authenticity,' as Mark Fisher states, 'the most convincing of signs that you were 4 Real.'

If we are all melancholic, as Baudrillard writes, then what comes after melancholy? Suicide? Overdose?

In many ways, the only way for Capitalist (Hyper)Realism to become real – to thoroughly mythologise itself as the only system left to us – so to speak – it must die spectacularly in the simulation of its death; another guarantee of authenticity, to disappear when it still has more to say, to embody its mode of disappearance – to haunt us. As such, the praxis of late capitalism accelerates towards this thirst for annihilation from which it can affirm a mythological status.

'When I die, you'll love me...'

In Baudrillard's 'Forget Foucault'[8], Sylvere Lotringer provides a fascinating insight; 'Traditional societies had no history, but they had a mythology; we're discovering now that history may have been our mythology.'

Without the mythologies of history as an operative referent – mythologies that find themselves increasingly attacked as systems of construction and belief, namely constructions of the powerful, capitalism looks towards its death for justification. The performative credibility of late capitalism's death drive is what Ted Kaczynski might have called a neat trick of the system[9], since, as Baudrillard responds to Lotringer, 'credibility alone is what gives things meaning,' the element that keeps us 'trapped in the imaginary.'

(つ◉◡◉)つ

Viewed from this Baudrillardian perspective, it seems a person trapped inside the realms and operative workings of the imaginary can only begin to disintegrate. Here, we observe the deterrence of the actual by way of the virtual. Speaking with Gus' older brother, David Peisner writes how Oskar Åhr

– Sad Boy Aesthetics –

'believed that the Xanax-popping, death-obsessed lothario of Peep's songs was merely a persona. Peep himself would draw that distinction,' Peisner concludes, 'later telling a friend that "Lil Peep is not well, but Gus is fine."' Nevertheless, Oskar admits, 'Over time, the line between the two seemed to disappear.'

(つ◕‿◕)つ

Someone once told me about a person they knew who, after a long day at work, would go home, open a bottle of Casillero del Diablo, and listen to Morrissey's early work. Despite ongoing fluctuations and segregations in public opinion – which is perhaps a part of the aesthetic itself – Morrissey represents, in the simplest terms, an 'OG sad boy'[10].

Morrissey instigates, in many ways, a tradition of androgynous young men who embody the melancholic; here, I am talking about how depressed I am, how nobody understands me, how alienation and limerence can come to define our experience in the world. (I would also like to add, early on, how this sad boy aesthetics is a gendered form in name only; other than this, it is a totally non-gendered style.)

If Casillero del Diablo is the drink you pair with Morrissey's earlier work, I wonder – most evenings – if there exists, somewhere, a drink you could pair with the early twenty-first century soundscapes of Peep. Immediately, the answers seem obvious enough, and yet it seems almost necessarily obvious not to be white wine, AriZona iced tea, nor cheap liquor on ice. After some consideration, we might consider the ideal drinks pairing as the canned juice James Sunderland finds in a decrepit hallway on the bottom floor of an apartment block in 'Silent Hill 2'.[11]

Thinking about it now, the ideal fans of Lil Peep, already saturated with authentic vibe check levels of sad boy aesthetic, would be James and Maria, the playable protagonists from 'Silent Hill 2', and 'Silent Hill 2: Born from a Wish'. Maria, the protagonist of that later side-story scenario – and major character of the main story of 'Silent Hill 2' – represents the total embodiment of the recurrent 'ghost girl' imagery which features heavily in the lyricism of Lil Peep's music. This is to jump the gun on lyrical analysis, since we should first define the parameters of what it means to occupy a place like Silent

Hill.

Silent Hill is a trashed world, and for many listeners, Lil Peep's music is trash too. Whilst the kneejerk reaction is to defend against this position, to say, hand on heart, that Lil Peep's music definitely isn't trash, I'm tempted to reframe trash as a positive occurrence, which is to say, give it power, because this isn't about proving a point, this isn't to say Lil Peep's music isn't worthless trash in a world where everything might as well be worthless trash. This is all to say how something can be said about the inherent nature of 'Trash Aesthetics', and how these may coalesce.

In regards to trash aesthetics, I will recall to mind the book, 'Inferno, Volume 1: The Trash Project'[12] by cultural theorist, Ken Hollings, who lays out, in this title, 'some basic principles for a Trash Aesthetics.' Here, the 'cynical poetry' of trash comes to represent the 'fault line running through our values and prejudices.' Hollings points to the history of trash 'as a strategy of resistance, as a refuge for creativity and a radical subversion of the ordinary...' Trash becomes, in this genealogy of 1960s culture, from Flash Gordon to the emergence of dirty movies, 'understood in mythological terms as a form of cultural hell – [...] immediately tragic, riddled with fatal flaws and satiric play, unloosening lust and grim self-knowledge.'

Hollings seems to adequately describe the artistry of Lil Peep, here. Mallgoth sincerity 'as an individual state of becoming – a striving towards a final condition which is only made possible by embracing the horror of disintegration.' Trash, conceptualised as an aesthetic hell, is full of sinners; 'the sinners in my aesthetic Hell' Hollings writes, 'are not there because they deserve to be, but because it suits them – they are more comfortable in their infernal circle than anywhere else.' 'Trash', like music, it seems, 'will always implicate you.' According to Hollings, it doesn't care – 'It forces me to admit that I am the product of a dirty and prohibitive culture.'

Initially, there is something dirty and prohibitive about enjoying any SoundCloud Rap, let alone an artist like Lil Peep, who developed thoroughly mainstream appeal – co-opted appeal, no less. Take, for example, my first ever experience with Yung Lean's 'Ginseng Strip 2002'[13]. Both repulsive and attractive, it is dirty and prohibitive to say you enjoy that song, let alone play it to your loved ones, and yet later manifestations of that vision, the 2020 album, 'Starz'[14], for example, develops gradually and obviously as an original work of genius.

And yet the desecration of something remains; it informs at the aesthetic level, even as we chart the migration away from SoundCloud towards Spotify and YouTube, and so on. Moreover, it is not unfair to mention how early contenders of the Cloud Rap aesthetic, Yung Lean's 'Kyoto'[15] and 'Yoshi City'[16], for example, which seem less about SoundCloud these days and more about YouTube – and more so with later entries like 'Violence + Pikachu'[17], existing within a 'personal form of discourse', as Hollings writes, only through an 'ability to evade rational and categorical thought.'

In an interview with Kerwin Frost[18], Yung Lean talked about filming the video for 'Ginseng Strip 2002' as 'a regular Tuesday after school' where friends and music associates took turns with the camera. Music producer, Yung Sherman, known contemporarily for his dreamy beats was 'hood famous' at the time, according to Lean, who later added his memetic lyricism to beats produced by both Sherman and Gud, the final member of the collective that came to be known as Sad Boys. (Yung Lean would later have the words 'Sad Boys' tattooed across his chest with flamboyant, gothic lettering.)

'So anyway, we had my parent's basement in the apartment building', Lean tells Frost, 'we took all of the stuff out and we put computers up, and we were just there, you know – *living in our made-up world.*'

In many ways, Sad Boy culture, the aesthetics that it produces from this landscape of 'trickle-down economy of waste' where, to use Hollings' phrasing, 'the Internet has become a vast, ever-expanding Trash pile' is to find a fruition in the ontologies of a hyperreal order thoroughly divorced from any sense of actuality – after all, sad boy aesthetics must occupy this *made up world*.

It is post-ironic too, existing, similarly to Hollings' Trash Aesthetics, as an aesthetic that comes to exist 'both with and without irony at the same time.' There are worse things than pessimism, as there are worse things than pure irony, after all, what is irony without humour? You can only ever free yourself from cynicism and despair by meeting it half way. This is at the heart of all sad boy aesthetics which acknowledge moral and emotional wrongdoings as ontologically positioned. Nonetheless, this is sadness unplugged and disconnected from any fixed origins – dissociated – developing from a moral order deterred by the virtual spaces that fail to love us back; 'an embodiment not of love' Hollings writes, 'but of a certain fascination with its absence...'

Obsessed with this absence of love, Lil Peep's artistry, the lyrics and visuals he produced in his short lifetime embody the infectious appeal of 'trash' and sadness, and as Hollings suggests, 'in its leering, misshapen and compromising way,' such aesthetics may be, in any small way, 'actually worth protecting.'

(つ◉⌣◉)つ

Long after his death, notable remixes of Lil Peep's 'Benz Truck'[19], 'Save That Shit'[20] and 'Star Shopping'[21] are uploaded to the YouTube account ＴＲＡＳＨ 新 ドラゴン paired with anime aesthetics from 'Tokyo Ghoul' and 'Beyond the Boundary'. These videos will be broadcast to 2.92 million subscribers.

(つ◉⌣◉)つ

Initially, Lil Peep becomes a representation of a human wreckage possessed with a tragic disposition. If 'Silent Hill 2' is a trashed world full of human wreckages, then James Sunderland develops, perhaps, as a protagonist wanting to find his wife in a ghostly dimension where his consciousness cannot free himself from an ideal representation of a feminine other; a 'ghost girl', quite literally, 'born from a wish.' It should be noted here how many of the characters who come to occupy a place like Silent Hill do so 'because it suits them – they are more comfortable' here, after all, in this 'Infernal circle...'

In retrospect, a game released in 2001 will always drip with a certain degree of trashy appeal. Bad voice acting and polygons resonate with a certain level of nostalgia that will only come to inform audience sensitivities at a later time. The occupation of irony as something which is both 'present and absent at the same time' is also withstanding, not only in a game like 'Silent Hill 2', but more broadly across the horror genre in general – from movies, games, literature, and so on.

Nevertheless, this is less about horror as a form of categorisation and more about James Sunderland and Maria as the ideal manifestations of Lil Peep's audience or, at least, as emblematic for the themes that his lyricism deals with. In this case, who are these people, and what do they really represent?

'In my restless dreams, I see that town...' a letter reads, delivered to James Sunderland and written by his late wife, Mary, who promises to meet her husband in Silent Hill, at a location she describes as the couple's 'special place.' James believes Mary is dead – ergo, the letter develops as a mysterious entity within itself, a product of an elsewhere world. 'I wrote a letter for you', Lil Peep sings, 'but you didn't write back.' In the twenty-first century, letters themselves become products of an elsewhere world, they possess a certain hauntological distance between the sender of the message, and the message received. This sentimentality adequately explains the persistence of letters in a technologically accelerated landscape which cannot seem to replicate all of the nuances and subtleties of human interaction.

In many ways, Lil Peep's music possesses a similar sentimentality, at times, reframed and readdressed in new and old ways. There is a hauntological element inside the dysfunctional hybridity of genre splicing. The hybridity of such genre composition, the blending of 90s punk pop/emo with hip-hop, for example, provides a way back to the past, and yet remains an incomplete vision, a thoroughly dysfunctional artistry.

The absence of its causation, nonetheless, the affected melancholy and the juxtaposition of depression with the mirror of depression, which is to say the 'manic elements' – particularly within the lyrics themselves – remains almost entirely unexplored. We know Lil Peep feels alone – but we don't know why. Recall the mysterious appeal of James' letter. Similarly, these lyrics resonate with listeners who cannot seem to locate the origins of their own depression/mania in anything external. As such, many of Lil Peep's lyrics deal with the destructive and problematic forms which can make a person feel temporarily sedated. It is music as the cohabitation of downers and uppers. Similar to a place like Silent Hill, Lil Peep comes to represent a world that is both comforting and disturbing at the same time. It develops as an overdose you're happy to fall into, the mists and drizzle of its downer haze[22] manifesting with Lynchian dynamism.

In 2018, YouTuber, AesirAesthetics[23], uploaded a five-hour long video analysis of 'Silent Hill 2' which details everything from game design to player mechanics. Within this analysis, he points to the Lynchian nature of the town, alongside other influences such as Fyodor Dostoevsky's 'Crime and Punishment'.

I want to use this phrasing as a segue into discussing both the Lynchian dynamics of the aesthetics discussed here – the sad boy aesthetic itself – alongside Lil Peep as a similar 'heroic auteur', working within the same remits of originality and self-possession. This is not to compare David Lynch with Lil Peep per se, but rather to suggest, in the phrasing of David Foster Wallace on the movie 'Blue Velvet', that 'what the really great artists do is they're entirely themselves. They've got their own vision, their own way of fracturing reality, and that if it's authentic and true, you will feel it in your nerve endings.'[24]

In the article, 'David Lynch Keeps His Head', Wallace refers to the 'academic definition' of the Lynchian as a term that can come to refer 'to a particular kind of irony where the very macabre and the very mundane combine in such a way as to reveal the former's perpetual containment within the latter.' The fact that Silent Hill takes place in an American township is fascinating to me. What's more, the structures of that township, the nightclubs and apartments, for example, are either laid bare, contaminated with a sticky Lovecraftian mire, or feature the banality of television sets and neon lights, which seem both inexplicably bizarre and perfectly reasoned at the same time.

'I've noted since 1986 (when Blue Velvet was released) that a good 65 percent of the people in metropolitan bus terminals between the hours of midnight and 6 A.M. tend to qualify as Lynchian figures-grotesque,' Wallace writes, 'enfeebled, flamboyantly unappealing, freighted with a woe out of all proportion to evident circumstances ... a class of public-place humans I've privately classed, via Lynch, as "insistently fucked up."'

One thing I've come to notice about the progenitors of sad boy aesthetics is their proximity to these public-places, their

— Sad Boy Aesthetics —

occupation of these 'non-places' – to use the term coined by Marc Augé[25]. In many ways, this aesthetic is born from these peculiar spaces of late capitalism.

Within 'The Slow Cancellation of the Future', Fisher recalls the British television series 'Sapphire and Steel'.

> 'One aim of Sapphire and Steel was to transpose ghost stories out of the Victorian context and into contemporary places, the still inhabited or the recently abandoned. In the final assignment, Sapphire and Steel arrive at a small service station. Corporate logos – Access, 7 Up, Castrol GTX, LV – are pasted on the windows and the walls of the garage and the adjoining café. This 'hallway place' is a prototype version of what the anthropologist Marc Augé will call in a 1995 book of the same title, 'non-places' – the generic zones of transit (retail parks, airports) which will come to increasingly dominate the spaces of late capitalism.'

'Who you worship when you're all alone?' Yung Lean sings on 'Acid at 7/11'[26], 'Acid at 7/11 (In the rain, in the rain) / I'm so gone.' The lyrics and title referring to 'your go-to convenience store for food, snacks, hot and cold beverages, gas and so much more.'[27] There is something unnervingly terrifying about convenience stores where 'the very macabre and the very mundane combine in such a way as to reveal the former's perpetual containment within the latter.'

It is a profoundly hallucinogenic realisation, coming to understand the human cohabitation of non-places as inferring dream reality. I have walked around a shopping mall, for example, and felt '"insistently fucked up."' 'Link at the gas stop...' Bladee raps on the track, 'Obedient'[28], featuring ECCO2K. For a prescient example of 'non-places' and their use within the aesthetic, refer to the music video for 'Obedient' where the mise en scène is exclusively one of car parks, a convenience store, and what appears to be an Amazon warehouse juxtaposed with the waves and strobing of an ocean by night.

Another instance of this 'non-place' cohabitation could be taken from the posthumous release of Peep's '4 Gold Chains'[29], featuring Clams Casino, where we observe a recording of the artist getting '"insistently fucked up"' on a street in London, where the lights of a twilight world glimmer in the distance.

Yung Lean's '7/11', and Bladee's 'gas stop', and with similar dimensional qualities, locations such as the 'strip club' and 'store' which feature in Peep's 'Beat It'[30], for example, become representative of Marc Augé's 'banal utopias' where '…the passive joys of identity loss,' are captured through hyper-hallucinogenic experiences of crude, highly simulated worlds. What reigns here, as Augé writes, is 'the urgency of the present moment' the sense of 'intersecting participation' where the 'space of non-place creates neither singular identity nor relations; only solitude, and similitude'.

Silent Hill is a virtual town that has been entirely regulated to the dimension of the non-placed – which is to also say absolutely nothing about the character Maria, other than to highlight her origins as a manifestation of the solitude that engulfs her.

(つ◕‿◕)つ

I first wanted to make the comparison between Lil Peep and the Nietzschean conception of the tragic disposition – and yet there can be no Dionysian affirmation of life.[31] Tragedy suggests catharsis. Lil Peep embodies tragedy *without* catharsis, where the pain lingers, demanding almost constant visitation. This is the haunting residue that comes to locate itself within the landscape of the sad boy aesthetic.

In paradoxical terms, through this elegiac and aesthetic form we are almost never entirely liberated and yet we are unknowingly suffocated beneath a temporaneous sedation. 'You take yourself seriously, stop', Bladee sings on the 2020 track, 'Reality Surf'[32] produced by whitearmor and Gud, 'Listen to your heart / Mirror, mirror, the reflection of the law / I just wanna show you something new…'

What I am now proposing is the death of Nietzsche's Dionysian and the Apollonian dichotomy, which requires an update for a new coded world where only reflections can now exist. Our world no longer encompasses the grand oppositions of logic and madness, for example. Today, nihilism reflects nihilism. Here, nihilism can only play with itself – and yet the nihilism remains hopeful (active), in thoroughly optimistic terms: 'From a situation in which nothing can happen' Mark Fisher writes in 'Capitalist Realism'[33], 'suddenly anything is possible again.'

James Sunderland is only ever a reflection of Maria, and vice versa. In this case, forgetting Nietzsche, we should observe James Sunderland and Maria from 'Silent Hill 2' as adequate replacements for the Dionysian and the Apollonian dichotomy since these characters come to represent one and the same aesthetic. They reveal the differentia, the play of opposites as illusory constructs. In the dissolution of the dichotomy, sad boy aesthetics charts the dissipation of diagnosis and symptom into one aesthetic form.

Both James and Maria, despite some superficial differences, (the embodiment of masculine and feminine elements), exist as terminally melancholic, as does you-know-who. This is all to say that Lil Peep's artistry does not affirm life, either. We are *collectively* melancholic, and here lies, perhaps, the revolutionary potential. On the other hand, maybe this sad boy aesthetic is paradoxical in provisional terms, offering only haunting refrains to a bygone world where we weren't all so dissociated from the causation of our miseries.

'To love someone is to isolate him from the world…'

Jean Baudrillard, Fatal Strategies

PART II: THE WAY I SEE THINGS:

From Lil Peep to the Hyperreal

— Sad Boy Aesthetics —

(っ◕‿◕)っ

One thing I enjoy about an unofficial YouTube upload of star shopping[34] is the anime aesthetic accompaniment that looks taken from a Studio Ghibli animation, or failing that an aesthetic taken from an early, turn of the millennium anime, something like 'Chobits'[35], which is ultimately an anime about loneliness and connection.

Something can be said about the cohabitation of the anime aesthetic with contemporary trends in music, from early lo-fi hip-hop to cloud rap and even vaporwave, at times, which seems to be more about capturing a certain emotional or visual period than anything else. (In an effort towards full disclosure, I was once banned from a vaporwave aesthetics messageboard for posting anime.)

Anime is primarily an aesthetics concerned with both sentimentality and pop culture, connecting with a generation raised on cartoon television, long before the internet was readily available, and the only way to watch anything remotely interesting was to stay up until 3AM channel surfing, where you might stumble onto a late night showing of 'Princess Mononoke'[36] or 'Ghost in the Shell'[37] or 'Sexcetera'. The whole nature of the anime aesthetic recalls the hypnogogic states we found ourselves in as young people, perhaps, it is even hauntological in the way it refers to 'the persistence and return of things from the past as in the manner of ghosts.'

There are exactly two moments from my youth that I remember with great fondness. One is a conversation I had with a group of older kids from a film studies class in which we had a deep and prevailing conversation about the merits of the chef's salad in Wong Kar-wai's 'Chungking Express'[38], and whether or not it was appropriate to say we enjoyed, as human beings, canned pineapple over fresh pineapple.

I remember distinctly falling in love for the first time, in that moment, with a girl expressing her love for canned pineapple, and the entire class, hostile and forthcoming, expressing their utter distaste for her, because how could a human being not prefer fresh pineapple. Nonetheless, this girl, beautiful in her conviction, remained adamant that canned pineapple was the superior choice, and whilst I remained silent at the time, I could not help but agree with her entirely, persuaded away from the merits of fresh pineapple towards the strange and alluring qualities of canned pineapple that seemed to be more about saving something beautiful and sweet from the destructive passages of time.[39]

I can also pinpoint the exact moment in my life, late at night, when I turned the television set from Melinda Messenger to Richard O'Brien, from Challenge TV to Challenge TV +1, to some obscure movie channel where I'd watch Hayao Miyazaki's 'Princess Mononoke' for the very first time, watch the young prince, Ashitaka, walk through a forest of tree sprites, ghostly and phantasmal, lacking any semblance of reality, and feeling, momentarily, completely and utterly dissociated from myself, and every one of my concerns, like staring up at a night sky of stars. 'Look at the sky tonight, all of the stars have a reason', Lil Peep sings with emotional resonance, 'A reason to shine, a reason like mine and I'm fallin' to pieces…'

Moving forward, we can say the track is demonstrative of the artist's natural tendency towards the ballad form as exploring intimate relationships, which is to also say, a song that develops as a beautifully melodic composition.

(つ◕‿◕)つ

The official video for Save That Shit[40] begins with a memorial: 'In loving memory of my son, Gus.' As such, the footage that accompanies the pop-esque vibes of the track become thoroughly recontextualised through the lens of death, which makes the otherwise banal interactions with his fanbase, for example, increasingly poignant and sad.

One thing that strikes me about the official music video is the prevalence of hotel rooms and hotel corridors. Something can be said about the nature of hotel rooms as totally creepy and weird places – non-places that you sleep and dream in – and wake up and have obscenely calorific breakfasts and do things that no normal person does, like sit in a sauna for ten to fifteen minutes at 8AM with a hangover. At a hotel in Liverpool, I once made a Bloody Mary at the 'Bloody Mary Self-Service Bar' located beside a pile of all-butter croissants, not because this had anything to do with any normal morning routine, but simply because the option was available to me.

Two things I enjoy doing at hotels is 1) checking for a

bible 2) reading the room-service menu. It should be noted that neither of these activities have anything to do with me as a person. Nonetheless, these things feature prominently in my experiences with hotel rooms, and will likely be one of those strange and inexplicable interests I will pursue until the occurrence of my own death at the hands of God knows who or what.

(つ◕‿◕)つ

An article published by Vice in 2016[41] described Lil Peep with the characteristically hipsterian disdain you would expect from a magazine that seemed to treat everything that walked on God's green earth through the lens of a snide, ironic distance. 'His songs are about doing cocaine, wanting to commit suicide,' Drew Millard writes, 'and talking to girls about cocaine and suicide.' Because there is a whole lot to comprehend in lyrics explicitly tied to cocaine and suicide, the whole aesthetic led cringe journalism to ask if Lil Peep's music was 'brilliant or stupid as shit.' They likely decided on stupid as shit because how could anything remotely sincere be anything other than stupid as shit.

A similar question would be asked in 1996, when David Foster Wallace came to interrogate the genius of David Lynch's Avant Garde film making. 'It's hard to tell whether the director's a genius or an idiot.' Wallace would note, 'This, for me, is part of his fascination.' The power of careful writing, Wallace's New Sincerity, for example, demonstrated how you could call someone a 'creepy person', yet remain almost entirely conscientious, especially if you'd previously described something of that person as 'creepy and moody and sexy and cool…'

'Lynch's movies are inarguably creepy,' Wallace would write, 'and a big part of their creepiness is that they seem so personal.' Perhaps this creepiness draws breath through Lynch's 'penchant for creepy small towns', whereby finetuned exposé can develop through personal experiences of the banal colliding with the perpetual horror of existence.

One thing I personally enjoy doing is listening to Lynch, an otherwise calm individual, mimic the voices of the insane. 'There might be something about his calm that's a little creepy – one tends to think of really high-end maniacs being oddly calm,' Wallace writes, considering the ways in which 'Hannibal Lecter's pulse rate stays under 80 as he bites somebody's tongue out.'

In the 2016 documentary, 'David Lynch: The Art Life'[42], Wallace's heroic auteur mimics, on occasion, the voices of at least two or three insane people with such perfect and terrifying accuracy it is almost as if these voices perpetually exist within himself. At the very least, we know Lynch, perhaps as a boy, perhaps as a young man, has really heard these voices.

'If the word sick seems excessive, substitute the word creepy.' Wallace suggests. 'A kind and simple way to put it is that Lynch's movies seem to be expressions of certain anxious, obsessive, fetishistic, oedipally arrested, borderlinish parts of the director's psyche, expressions presented with little inhibition or semiotic layering, i.e., presented with something like a child's ingenuous (and sociopathic) lack of self-consciousness.' Whilst a perfect description of Lynch's work as a whole, Wallace may have also inadvertently formed a perfect elucidation of the sad boy aesthetic operating with a similar ingenuity. At the very least, this adequately summarises the expressions presented by Lil Peep's psyche. These are the expressions of someone whose music is not categorically stupid, but rather exists without the slightest desire for semiotic layering, remaining, at all times, entirely obsessive and borderline and seemingly authentic.

One of my favourite interviews with David Lynch was conducted with 'Noisey'[43] Creative Director, Eddy Moretti. In this interview the magazine's irony for irony's sake meets irony without humour in the form of David Lynch. At the beginning of the interview, Moretti pulls out a glossy issue of his magazine, I suppose, asking Lynch 'the most important question of all, of course – what do you think of Vice?'

David Lynch replies, calmly and simply: 'Vice is modern…' because this is David Lynch, after all, and David Lynch doesn't give a fuck.

'What do you mean… modern?' Moretti asks, frowning.

'Well, look at this cover.' Lynch looks towards the camera, brandishing the magazine. 'It's a modern cover. It sends out a certain kind of message that it's – umm – hip – and modern, and you're going to find out stuff, you know, when you read this.'

— Sad Boy Aesthetics —

Four years later, one of the things you could find out from the magazine was whether or not Lil Peep's music was 'brilliant or stupid as shit.' Referring to Lil Peep's Crybaby[44], Drew Millard writes, 'If you ignore the lyrics' actual content (which oscillates between asinine and laughable) and instead focus on their construction, you start to understand why you haven't stopped listening to Lil Peep even though you also think his music is virtuosically moronic.'

Asinine because you're incapable of understanding what it means to exhibit a disposition of pointlessness, I suppose, and laughable because that's the only way to treat anything worthwhile or sincere when you're desperately clawing at hip cynicism. There is almost zero consideration to the fact that if Lil Peep's music was so pathologically sick, then what could be said about his creative expression as a product of an even sicker culture?

A few years later, Vice awards Lil Peep 'Artist of the Decade'[45] – 'He didn't cloud his feelings in metaphor or wordplay, he simply said what he was feeling—and most often, he was feeling bad.' Colin Joyce concludes, 'It's an approach that caused this very website to wonder early in his career if he was "stupid as shit."'

Wherever you go, wherever you look, the world and its people are full of strange justifications. Listening to a journalist trying to be sincere, justifying a position in retrospect, is like listening to a replicant trying to pass the Voight-Kampff test from 'Blade Runner'[46]. You're in a *desert*, walking along in the sand when all of a sudden you look down and see a tortoise, Colin. It's crawling towards you. You know what a turtle is? You reach down and you flip the tortoise on its back, Drew.

(つ◉‿◉)つ

A sun sets over a warm ocean. A flock of gulls pass a pastel sky haemorrhaging with the hues of titanium white and the lighter shades of alizarin crimson. These emotive scenes converge with home footage in a fan made video for Lil Peep's track Right Here[47] uploaded to YouTube in 2018. The care and patience elicited into producing these fan edits should stand as a testament to Gus' legacy.

A lot can be said about Lil Peep invoking his own

relationship towards what Mark Fisher might have called a depressive ontology. 'Depressive ontology is dangerously seductive...' Fisher writes, 'As the depressive withdraws from the vacant confections of the lifeworld, he unwittingly finds himself in concordance with the human condition [...] he sees himself as a serial consumer of empty simulations, a junky hooked on every kind of deadening high[.]' There is little difference between the 'depressive iron certainty' that Fisher located in the lyricism and artistry of Ian Curtis' 'Joy Division' and tracks like 'Right Here', for example, that drip with a certain 'fatalism', in the words of Fisher, the voice of the already dead, 'an appalling state of suspended animation, death-within-life.'

'Baby how you doing?' Peep asks, inverting the expectations of a depressed person who we always expect will want to talk only about themselves, and their own sadness. His voice remains genuinely inquisitive. 'I know you not doing the best but I'm here, I'll always be here.' There is a poignant self-awareness from the mind of the artist, especially, as to why we are listening to this track since – like Peep – we feel like shit too. 'Tell me if you need me and call me if you feelin' alone 'cause I'm here, I'm always right here' and 'I'll wait right here', he tells us.

Where is the 'here' Peep is talking about other than within the intimate moment of the musical experience itself? Music is a shared expression of feelings channelled between the artist and the listening audience. The 'here' in this song, particularly, develops as an intimacy saved from total diminishment, a hologram rendition that can provide – even when he's gone – a level of abstract interaction.

(つ◕‿◕)つ

A track like Hellboy[48] represents early indications of Lil Peep's movement towards the fallen angel imagery. In an interview with one of the most 'influential and enigmatic electronic musicians of the early 21st Century', Mark Fisher asked Burial about angels.

'Mates laugh at me because I like whale songs.' Burial responds. 'But I love them, I like vocals to be like that, like a night cry, an angel animal.' This admission aided Fisher's interpretation of Burial as an audio vision of mutilated angels, and the cities they come to occupy. 'Burial agrees, 'wanting an angel to be watching over you, when there's nowhere to go and all you can do is sit in McDonalds late at night, not answering your phone.'

'What is suppressed in postmodern culture is not the Dark but the Light side.' Fisher later writes, 'We are far more comfortable with demons than angels. Whereas the demonic appears cool and sexy, the angelic is deemed to be embarrassing and sentimental.' Contemporary societies present angelic qualities as insincere and disingenuous, channelling an image that fails to acknowledge any shadow.

Here, Fisher's words recall a moral dichotomy that can no longer exist within the landscapes of postmodern relativism, where there can be no angels. Even so, angels have always existed in a world between worlds, inherently compromised by material realms. Why else would God send angels – if it wasn't for the fear of becoming compromised?

Nonetheless, '… heavenly fire no longer falls on corrupted cities…' Baudrillard writes in 'Simulacra and Simulations', and whilst the referential dichotomy of heaven and hell has been thoroughly liquidated in secular living, there remains a hauntological refrain captured in the iconography of angels and demons.

(つ◑‿◐)つ

'Bump Lil Peep, when I die I'mma haunt you…'

Music is a type of haunting. I realise this may seem like a trite and banalizing statement, and yet it always comes to mind when I consider a track like Haunt U[49] which pertains to the elegiac qualities of Lil Peep's artistry. Some people cannot wait to die, and many of those same people, paradoxically speaking, are driven by an exhaustive guilt for feeling that way.

(つ◑‿◐)つ

In Teen Romance[50], we can trace the history of pop punk and its relationship to the ballad form, fusing it with genre hybridity to create some of the nicest acoustic guitars ever sampled onto a rap track. (I'm not even sure this is a rap track – what is it?) Ballads are sentimental or romantic songs concerned with storytelling. One thing they don't tell you early on in life is how you can go through your entire existence and only ever experience romance vicariously. Somethings are never talked about enough, like this, for example, the prevalence of romantic comedies that make up for both romance and humour's distinct absence in *real* life.

(つ◕‿◕)つ

Something should be said about the erasure of Lil Tracy from Peep's later works, especially on post-humorous releases that feature artists other than his onetime best friend and music associate. I don't really care about the public falling out between Lil Tracy and Lil Peep, and one can't help but feel like it played into a marketing gimmick, the legacy of rivalries between two similarly positioned emo rap artists. What better narrative than rivals who were once friends?

Nonetheless, the tendency for music write-ups to focus exclusively on the white artist, in this case, whilst erasing other important voices is inherently problematic, especially when the music, the legacy of hip-hop itself, has a debt to the Black experience. This is more a criticism on the nature of magazine criticism in general, which remains dominated by privileged voices often focused solely on PR and marketing.

These criticisms should not extend to Lil Peep, however, who – even from Tracy's perspective – was always willing to share the vision, and allow space for collaborations in an emergent scene that often went beyond racial boundaries. This is one of the achievements of music that exists outside of the corporate mainstream – and within hip-hop, especially – since it doesn't matter who you are, or what you've come from; all that matters is your lyricism, in this case, and your ability to connect on a beat.

One of the greatest synergies between artists was produced on tracks like Your Favorite Dress[51] featuring Lil Tracy. The public falling out between Peep and Tracy should be taken as evidence for the genuineness – the authenticity – of their relationship, and by extension, the music they made together. A part of the tragedy of death – if we can even call it that – will always concern the loss of creative potential, and a part of that loss will, in addition, stem from never getting to see Tracy and Peep find their moment of reconciliation.

(つ◉‿◉)つ

I am conflicted about the track Yesterday[52] which features a sample from the band, Oasis. Every kid who grew up with swirl textured ceilings had the lyrics from 'Wonderwall'[53] drilled into them since birth. (As a side note, I once got into a conversation with the folks at the London Review Bookshop because they didn't understand how people ordered food in a greasy spoon cafeteria, and they needed the lyrics from The Street's 'Don't Mug Yourself'[54] explaining to them.) That being said, so much of a certain class experience can be captured in those 'Wonderwall' lyrics. I recall to mind the lines that appear right before the hook; 'There are many things that I / Would like to say to you but I don't know how…'

At the same time, I can appreciate the resentment many feel towards Oasis, especially for something as overheard and overprescribed as 'Wonderwall', whose best rendition can now be heard on the night train from Manchester Piccadilly Station. There is something wry about Lil Peep's alternate version, however, which seems to mock the boy at the party who is keen to exhibit his entry level guitar skills for the perceived sensitivities of indie girls.

Everyone has heard that joke about as many times as they've heard 'Wonderwall', which seems to feature on anything remotely related to Cool Britannia. Full disclosure: I was once so drunk in a karaoke bar that I turned off someone's shitty rendition of that song. (I had many additional drinks bought for me after the fact.)

Oasis represents what Mark Fisher, in an interview with Andrew Broaks, called the 'depthless contemporary' of the '90s. '…the pseudo opposition between Blur and Oasis that was more sort of a battle between mediocre class stereotypes.' Fisher writes, 'Students slumming it, as Ian Penman put it about Blur, versus this utter neanderthal cartoon of the working class, as if they were the only options available.' Fisher's biggest criticism of Oasis wasn't necessarily the class stereotypes per se, but concerned, instead, the passage of cultural time away from a progression into a viable and happy future. The retro vibes found in Oasis, for example, were symptomatic of the termination of what Fisher termed 'popular modernism'.

– Alex Mazey –

The disappointment and mourning for this failed future were later captured in '00s Emo, I claim, a genre that seemed to go almost totally unrecognised by Fisher. Here's the thing, I love Saetia's 'A Retrospective', it's one of my favourite albums of all time, but I also enjoyed listening to My Chemical Romance's early work, which seemed to bridge the gap between commercially viable pop music and a vision that still spoke to people in emotive and meaningful ways.

The humorous element to Peep's 'Yesterday' comes in the total reframing of time itself, indicating how Oasis' 'Today', the promise of speaking truth to power in the here and now, for example, never actually materialised for anyone. 'Yesterday is not today, yesterday is not today', Peep chants like a mantra. 'Today is gonna be the day that I'm gonna come back to you / I know, I did a little blow and I never wrote back to you…'

The hauntological imagery of letter writing appears once again, and yet what is it that the we have come back to here, other than an additional litany of crimes; and what is a crime when everyone is complicit? The subconsciously borderline complicity with what we might have once called evil reveals everything you need to know about postmodern morality. The grotesque belch at the end of this track, in addition, probably tells you everything you need to know about how Peep really felt towards the anthemic potential of a song like 'Wonderwall'.

(つ◕‿◕)つ

'I feel like I'm a no one, that's what they told me / I'mma show ya, baby, I was chosen, ayy…' Lil Peep raps on Beamerboy[55] – a track that very much appeals to the themes imbued into sad boy aesthetics' association to and with hedonic melancholy. This variation of the melancholic experience is both an obvious variable in terms of the song's actual lyrical content, and the aesthetic form itself.

In terms of musical analysis, there remains some beautiful, deep reverberations at the beginning of this track, where we hear Peep talking about people hitting up his phone presumably because of his growing traction in the SoundCloud community at the time. One thing that struck me about the Lil Peep documentary, 'Everybody's Everything', pertained to the early live performances of this track in particular; a chaotic energy which seemed to possess an authentic, punk show vibe.

In her New Yorker article, 'Lil Xan and the Year in Sad Rap'[56], Carrie Battan writes that '"emorap" was once an answer to a crossword clue in the Times.' According to Battan, this emergent cohort of young rappers were 'more likely to worship Kurt Cobain or Marilyn Manson than Jay-Z or Kanye West'. A statement that appeared to ignore the registered melancholy of West's later albums, especially, which seemed to define the 21st century milieu with its all-consuming inertia of sadness. This is to say that "Emorap" owed an obvious debt to hip-hop as much as it owed anything to the genres of grunge, punk and emo.

'…it's perhaps in hip-hop', Mark Fisher once wrote[57], 'the genre that has been most oriented to pleasure over the past 20-odd years—where this melancholy has registered most deeply. Drake and Kanye West are both morbidly fixated on exploring the miserable hollowness at the core of super-affluent hedonism. No longer motivated by hip-hop's drive to conspicuously consume—they long ago acquired anything they could have wanted—Drake and West instead dissolutely cycle through easily available pleasures, feeling a combination of frustration, anger, and self-disgust, aware that something is missing, but unsure exactly what it is. This hedonist's sadness—a sadness as widespread as it is disavowed—was nowhere better captured than in the doleful way that Drake sings, "we threw a party/yeah, we threw a party," on Take Care's "Marvin's Room".'

I am inclined to agree with Fisher here, believing this melancholic hedonism exists as a prevalent force within contemporary hip-hop perhaps more than any other genre discussed in this text. Even the 'sad and desperate' landscape of 'pop culture hedonism' has become like a 'drug that we've hammered so much we've become immune to its effects.' Pop musicians have today produced an ideologically-charged soundscape of 'demands' and 'thin attempts', according to Fisher, operating as mere distraction 'from a depression that they can only mask, never dissipate.'

Nonetheless, the important and significant aspect acknowledged by Battan is this cohabitation of 'morbidity and mania' found in emo rap, a theme she tied to XXXTentacion's debut studio album, and later to the 'bratty melancholy' found on Lil Uzi Vert's single, 'xo tour llif3'[58]. Another ignorance in Battan's writing is revealed in the statement connecting 'emo rap' not to the 'invincibility' of hip-hop but with a new generation of rappers 'fixated on mortality.' The whole shtick of hip-hop was always about presenting your 'invincibility' in the face of your environment's hostility; the dangers of being Black in White America, for example. In this way, hip-hop was always about 'mortality'.

That being said, the distinguishing feature between today's hip-hop and the hip-hop of the ninety's era, for example, is certainly the elevation of what we should consider as a 'Popular Nihilism'. 'Nihilism, taken to an extreme that feels almost competitive, has become its own form of braggadocio.' Batten writes. This is nihilism less as 'braggadocio' and more as its own form of authenticity, I claim; an acknowledgement that nothing really matters within a culture that despises life, anyway. If hip-hop is concerned with authenticity, and presenting an authentic account of life, it becomes the genre most geared towards presenting the nihilism that lies at the heart of our modes of living today.

'Post Malone, a singer and rapper tangentially connected to the SoundCloud community, rose to the top of the Hot 100 toward the end of 2017 with "rockstar,"', Batten writes, 'a song that makes success sound as joyless as possible.' One thing that strikes me about Batten's writing is the sardonic inflections describing Post Malone as 'joyless', as she does here, to describing Peep's 'Beamerboy' as 'perhaps the most morbid song about luxury cars ever recorded.'

There is almost zero consideration to the fact that expressions of 'joylessness', 'morbidity', and 'bratty melancholy' in art and music, especially, could become exactly what audiences want from new aesthetic forms that might actually acknowledge a collective experience, rather than mask it, which is to also say, provide a much-needed sense of disclosure.

(つ◕‿◕)つ

The official video for Lil Jeep[59] has an a-ha 'Take On Me'[60] vibe throughout the video, where we see Peep becoming a stylised pencil-sketch animation version of himself. I was always a little concerned for English model and actress, Bunty Bailey in the 'Take On Me' video (which used a similar pencil-sketch aesthetic), since it was like the actress was experiencing a psychotic break from which we were observing in a sort of sick, voyeuristic way.

If it wasn't for the playful tune, a-ha's lead singer, Morten Harket's creepy wink from the black and white pages of the magazine would appear demonic, and the magazine would be sent away to Ed and Lorraine Warren for further inspection. Honestly, go and watch the video... Watch as Harket's arm emerges from the pages of the cartoon strip like it's a fucking horcrux. The terror on Bailey's face as she looks around the roadside café, before being dragged into the cartoon underworld remains a testament to just how much cocaine was snorted in the '80s.

What's so interesting is how Bailey succumbs almost instantaneously to the allure of this ghostly white hand. The moment this hallucinatory image emerges from the pages, she's happy to suspend her utter and total disbelief despite the fact that no one else in the café can see what's happening to her. In fact, as Bailey takes Harket's hand, the actress develops an almost 'Fuck it, why not?' expression that most people can only muster after three or four strawberry daiquiris. (Also, why does Harket look like a sweaty mechanic?)

Meanwhile, back in the roadside café, the waitress is vexed because she thinks Bunty Bailey has dipped on the bill when really she has been absorbed into the texture of an alternate universe. The waitress is really angry at the comic book for some reason. She trashes the comic book into a bin behind the counter which seemingly informs the reality inside the pencil-sketch animation, which somehow becomes even more nightmarish at this point. The couple are now being chased through a series of labyrinthine-white corridors by men wielding wrenches. Reaching a dead end, and clawing at the walls, Harket tears another whole in the fabric of his dimensional reality in order to facilitate Bailey's escape.

Bailey then materializes beside the trash can in the roadside café. Patrons of hot tea and coffee observe her flustered disposition from behind the safety of an espresso machine. No doubt, it remains a Kafkaesque room of inquisitive and questioning gazes. Bailey snags the comic strip, nonetheless, fleeing the audience of concerned onlookers. Back at home, in the solitude of her room, she watches Harket materialise from his alternative dimension, because he's looking for her, and because he loves her now, I guess. Harket now stands in the corridor of Bailey's house like a terminator teleported from the future.

The official video for this Lil Peep song doubles down on the absurdity of pencil-sketch animation by supplementing it with footage that looks taken from 'The Ring'[61] (2002) videotape that kills you in seven days.

As a side note, I love the line about the flip phone in this track since it calls to my mind a flip phone[62] that I once owned until the day I came home from working on a waterlogged building site and my mother, trying to help the best she could, put it in the washing machine by accident.

(つ◉‿◉)つ

'...Trash is culture retold as a joke', Hollings writes, '– and, like all jokes, it becomes a harbinger of doom.' I love this idea of comedy as a form of cataclysmic prophecy. I know happiness has absolutely nothing to do with comedy. It is a total fiction, you see, this notion of laughter having anything to do with happiness.

'Happy.' Arthur smirks. 'I haven't been happy one minute of my entire fucking life.' He breathes out cigarette smoke. 'You know what's funny? You know what really makes me laugh? I used to think that my life was a tragedy,' the professional clown smothers his adoptive mother beneath a pillow, '...but now I realise it's a fucking comedy.' He notes.

Something should be said about that scene from 'The Joker'[63] (2019), beginning with the title character, played by Joaquin Phoenix, framed behind the almost velvety-blue, stage-curtains of a hospital ward. 'The division between worlds was often marked by one of Lynch's frequently recurring visual motifs: curtains.' Mark Fisher writes in 'The Weird and The Eerie'[64], referring here, of course, to 'Blue Velvet'[65] (1986) and 'Twin Peaks'[66] – the magnum opus of Lynch's career.

'Curtains both conceal and reveal...' Fisher writes, referring to the ways in which curtains frame a scene, drawing audience attentions to the nature of the cinema screen itself. Curtains and holes become 'world-haemorrhaging', here, offering an architecture and a terrain subjected to 'chronic ontological

Sad Boy Aesthetics

subsidence' where 'dreams become taken for reality' and 'reality subsides into a dream.' The brilliance of Lynch's work has always been about the audience's inability to distinguish between the two. There is something inexplicably comical about this inability to differentiate reality from dreamworlds, which has almost nothing to do with happiness and almost everything to do with making the viewers feel thoroughly uncomfortable – misplaced – ontologically repositioned by its subsidence.

In an interview with literary critic, Larry McCaffery[67], David Foster Wallace paraphrased, I think, the Mexican poet, Cesar A. Cruz when he said 'good fiction's job was to comfort the disturbed and disturb the comfortable.' For art, this is best achieved in the realms of comedy, which is probably why so many critics found Wallace's 'Infinite Jest' to be a funny novel. I am reminded, also, of David Foster Wallace's 'Laughing with Kafka'[68], taken from a speech printed in Harper's Magazine in 1998: 'For me, a signal frustration in trying to read Kafka with college students is that it is next to impossible to get them to see that Kafka is funny...' Wallace continues:

'...the particular sort of funniness Kafka deploys is deeply alien to kids whose neural resonances are American. The fact is that Kafka's humor has almost none of the particular forms and codes of contemporary U.S. amusement. There's no recursive wordplay or verbal stunt-pilotry, little in the way of wisecracks or mordant lampoon. There is no body-function humor in Kafka, nor sexual entendre, nor stylized attempts to rebel by offending convention. No Pynchonian slapstick with banana peels or rapacious adenoids. No Rothish satyriasis or Barthish meta parody or arch Woody-Allen ish kvetching. There are none of the ba-bing ba-bang reversals of modern sitcoms; nor are there precocious children or profane grandparents or cynically insurgent coworkers. Perhaps most alien of all, Kafka's authority figures are never just hollow buffoons to be ridiculed, but are always absurd and scary and sad all at once...'

It is significant that Charlie Chaplin's 'Modern Times'[69] (1936) appears intertextually within 'The Joker' since it is here where we might observe the true nature of comedy, not as a reductive serotonin dump of happiness, not as something to make you feel good per se, but as a revealing force, a refrain against the desert of the real. Nothing about 'Modern Times' is happy either, but it is funny, and it is comical. When you really think about it, 'The Joker' is only a contemporary reimagining of Chaplin's 'Modern Times', which also happens to be my favourite movie of all time.

> 'Isn't life beautiful? I think that life is beautiful
> Wake up in the morning, now you doing the impossible
> Find out what's important, now you're feeling philosophical
>
> When I die, I'll pack my bags, move somewhere more affordable
> Isn't life horrible? I think that life is horrible
> You think she's adorable, she thinks that you're intolerable
>
> You think you can do it, but your chances are improbable
> Once you feel unstoppable, you run into an obstacle
> Isn't life comical? I think that life is comical…'

'Isn't life comical? I think that life is comical…' Peep raps on Life Is Beautiful[70] – one of my favourite tracks of all time, where the artist's lyrics could read like modern American poetry full of comedic wit, of a grandfather who doesn't want him, a tumour that might kill him, and worser still, a girl who doesn't want him, either. 'Kafka's comedy is always also tragedy,' David Foster Wallace writes, 'and this tragedy always also an immense and reverent joy.'

'There is hope,' Kafka writes, 'but not for us.'

(っ◉‿◉)っ

Lil Peep makes frequent, almost obsessive and maniacal reference to libidinal expressions. A track like About U[71] provides a principal example; 'Okay, I admit I wanna fuck you', Peep sings, 'But it doesn't change the way I feel about you…'

Morality represents a trans-political geography. Lyrics such as these configure reactionary drives against the schizophrenic moralising of our dominant ontologies, fixated both on an inherent relativity of morality and a dogmatic fanaticism with it. The libidinal impulse reveals the paradoxes that levitate within the uncharted peripheral of human experience.

One of the latent capacities of aesthetics is this ability to say absolutely nothing about morality, whilst contemporaneously exposing and disintegrating ethics as a product of cultural production.

(つ◉‿◉)つ

When I recall a track like Ghost boy[72], I want to focus almost exclusively on Maria from 'Silent Hill 2'. In many ways, Maria represents the ambience of Silent Hill – the presence of the town itself – which we already know possesses a Lynchian dynamic. (The banal collides with horror to reveal the perpetual horror of the banal.)

Compared to the stifling interiors of the domestic setting, hospitals and apartment blocks, and so on, the town is structured in a way that makes the exterior world feel almost comforting, even when the town possesses thoroughly otherworldly qualities; mists and inescapable monsters. (Otherworldly compared to what?)

In the first episode of 'Twin Peaks', the opening credits cut from ducks on a lake, (an outside, exterior), to a warped representation of ducks (or are they hunting dogs?) in the form a banal ornamental piece, sitting on a *vanity* table, (this ornamental arrangement is, on the other hand, situated in a domestic interior.) This can relate directly to a Baudrillardian analysis in relation to the four stages of sign-order. The two ducks on the pond are a reflection of a profound reality whilst the two-duck ornament forms an artificial representation, an unfaithful copy rendered in a modernist, aesthetic style that calls into question the nature of reality as representation.

These communicative simulacra, the ornament, in this case, structure the reality of domestic interiors full of fakery and artifice, (remember the vanity table?) which themselves attempt to structure exterior reality. Standing in comparison to the ecstatic communication of cities, I sometimes wonder if small town America, saturated with everyday banality, whilst also sitting in closer proximity to the 'natural world', hangs on the peripheral edges of the hyperreal.

This is what makes small towns so peculiar, perhaps; an unplaceable strangeness also captured in films like Edgar Wright's 'Three Flavours Cornetto trilogy' – to find a British comparison. Wright's series of films concern the undiscovered evil that lies behind artificial veneers, especially in instalments such as 'Hot Fuzz'[73] (2007) and 'The World's End'[74] (2013). Even so, these films are ultimately about wish fulfilment, a way to make the peculiarities of the hyperreal make sense. From myth to contemporary forms of mediation, monsters have always been the easiest way to do just that.

It is far scarier to imagine a world without monsters. It is an indifferent world, after all, where nothing cosmically monstrous awaits in the darkness; it seems there is only ever a profound absence. (Evil is the saviour's greatest joy since it confirms the existence of a mythological dichotomy, which is to say the referential interplay of good and evil.) This interpretation represents a thoroughly optimistic interpretation of absence as possessing any semblance of actuality. Nonetheless, absence is the volume of reality. The real is only ever what we make of it. *The simulacrum is true.*

Compare a town like Silent Hill to a town like Twin Peaks and you'll soon discover almost zero differences between the two. The peculiarities remain very much the same, here. Watch the opening credits of 'Twin Peaks' and then tell me there isn't something simultaneously comforting *and* disturbing, in addition, highlighting the dichotomy of comfort/discomfort as pure simulation, also. A second point of comparison might be located in their musical arrangements. Compare Twin Peaks' Instrumental Theme[75], produced by Angelo Badalamenti, to Silent Hill 2's soundtrack[76]. Many of these compositions are similarly positioned in their ability to reproduce the exact same mixed-state, mood regulation – a comfort that can be taken in the disturbing and the uncomfortable; an *undisturbing*.

'Ghosting'[77] is the practice of abruptly ending an intimate relationship with someone without explanation, whilst disappearing from all virtual and material means of communication. Lil Peep's obsession with ghost girls and ghosted love indicates a similar obsession with comfort within discomfort, the satisfaction one might feel towards feelings not of love, but of limerence, for example. There is something *undisturbing* about ghosted love, in this instance, the lost potential towards happiness or fulfilment indicating happiness or fulfilment as an achievable paradigm; a profound reality. This is essentially hauntological; the pathologizing of the hauntological experience towards aspects of the libidinal.

— Sad Boy Aesthetics —

This is all to say that ghosting relates to the perverse enjoyment of the sudden and abrupt failure of love to materialise.

Moreover, one of the most fascinating things about Maria from 'Silent Hill 2' is how she exists as a simulacrum. She is an 'unsatisfactory imitation or substitute' for James' wife, and yet somehow we come to enjoy Maria's presence in the game far more than we enjoy Mary's character since Mary has only ever felt absent – distant – coming to us in the form of a letter. Maria, by comparison, is existent, she *appears* as warm bodied, flesh and blood. This represents the perniciousness of the simulation which is always more satisfying than any sense of actuality.

(っ◉‿◉)っ

'Promise me it's real…' Lil Peep sings on Big City Blues[78] featuring Cold Hart. In terms of an analysis of the hyperreal, make of those lyrics what you will.

(っ◉‿◉)っ

When he was Nineteen[79], Lil Peep wanted to skip school, stay by the pool, take codeine, and write raps. When I was nineteen, I still wanted to study philosophy at Blackfriars College. Ten years later, and I continue to waste my potential as a human being by staying up late and noticing the synchronicities in the filmography of American film producer, Buzz Feitshans. For example, 'First Blood' (1982), 'Rambo: First Blood Part II' (1985), 'Rambo III' (1988), 'Total Recall' (1990) and 'Judge Dredd' (1995) all feature scenes that include 'The Coca-Cola Company'.[80]

(っ◉‿◉)っ

'What I am, I don't know. I am the simulacrum of myself.'
Jean Baudrillard

Something should be said about the transparency of the postmodern world. 'When I look at you / I can see right through…' Lil Peep sings on Me And You[81] featuring Cold Hart. 'For Baudrillard,' Professor Douglas Kellner writes in the 'Stanford Encyclopedia of Philosophy'[82], 'the "ecstasy of communication" means that the subject is in close proximity to instantaneous images and information, in an overexposed and transparent world […] an individual in a postmodern world becomes merely an entity influenced by media, technological experience, and the hyperreal.'

This is such a transparent actuality, such an easy to perceive truth, for lack of a better word, that it seems almost platitudinous to mention, here. However, '…the media, simulations, hyperreality, and implosion eventually came to obliterate distinctions between private and public, inside and outside, media and reality.' Kellner continues, 'Henceforth, everything was public, transparent, and hyperreal in the object world that was gaining in fascination and seductiveness as the years went by.'

We can now see, as the years went by, how Gustav Åhr became utterly saturated by the very public and mediated perceptions of himself as a 'Xanax-popping, death-obsessed lothario', to use David Peisner's words. In many ways, succumbing to the seductiveness of Lil Peep's identity was always going to materialise as a fatal strategy in a world that endorsed nihilism at its worst, and melancholic hedonism as its state of pre-eminence.

(つ◕‿◕)つ

It is a poignant and ephemeral experience to enjoy a track like Falling Down[83] featuring XXXTentacion when you consider the actuality of listening to two young men who are already dead. A similar experience can be felt on a track like Juice Wrld's 'Lucid Dreams'[84], for example.

Twenty-five years after its initial release, Juice Wrld would sample Sting's 'Shape Of My Heart'[85] on this track. A year later, Juice Wrld would die in an airport, aged twenty-one, from a drug-induced seizure. This death would coincide, of course, with the deaths of both XXXTentacion and Lil Peep occurring only a few years apart.

One thing that strikes me about Sting's 'Ten Summoner's Tales' is the melancholic disposition, the intertextuality of the speakers, the residue of Sting's earlier work in The Police, and so on. Interestingly enough, when Sting talks about the 'You', in those tracks, he is referring to himself, I

— Sad Boy Aesthetics —

claim. Arguably speaking, the Summoner in those tracks is summoning notions of 'Gordon Sumner', which stands in contrast to the very public persona of 'Sting', making it one of the more intimate albums of his career. In fact, a year after its release, 'Ten Summoner's Tales' was nominated for 'Album of the Year', losing the Grammy to the best-selling soundtrack album of all time, Whitney Houston's 'The Bodyguard'.

Nevertheless, in an article for The New York Times, 'Attention Shoppers: Internet Is Open'[86], Peter H. Lewis, would write how, 'From his work station in Philadelphia, Mr. Brandenburger logged onto the computer in Nashua, and used a secret code to send his Visa credit card number to pay $12.48, plus shipping costs, for the compact disk "Ten Summoners' Tales" by the rock musician Sting.' This would make Sting's 'Ten Summoners' Tales' the first item purchased over the Internet, by secure means, paving the way for the internet as we know it today.

'Ten Summoners' Tales', released in the early nineties, captured a milieu that would define a generation, full of hauntological awareness, and a trajectory away from the modernism that defined the twentieth century. The lyrics on the first track begin, 'You could say I lost my faith in science and progress / You could say I lost my belief in the holy Church / You could say I lost my sense of direction / You could say all of this and worse, but / If I ever lose my faith in you / There'd be nothing left for me to do…'

There is something of the Nietzschean-Dionysiac captured in these lyrics, despite the prevailing melancholia of later tracks, I claim, regarding Sting's undying faith in himself, a faith grounded, perhaps, in nostalgic recollections of places that no longer or never existed, where, 'the west wind moves upon the fields of barley…'

Even so, the trajectory of society twenty-five years later would manifest as a world where young musicians, shot in the street, or collapsing into drug abuse, would barely live past the age of twenty.

(つ◕‿◕)つ

Like so many of his finest tracks, 16 Lines[87] begins with an emotive guitar backing, grounding the music within the familiar landscapes of alternative rock and emo. 'Sixteen lines of blow and I'm fine...' Peep's characteristic voice emerges as a distant resounding, running as an accompaniment to this guitar progression. This is the signature opening to so many of these tracks, (similar openings can be observed on 'Beamer Boy' and 'Save That Shit', for example), which often demonstrate a complete and total mastery over the downbeat drop.

The piano chops enter the composition at around thirty-four seconds, providing a grounding release whilst simultaneously indicating a movement away from the more alternative rock elements, which reframes alternative rock – and the piano itself – as a conventional formulation. This adequately explains why Lil Peep's music provides something that initially feels quite familiar and comforting whilst developing towards an artistry that is ultimately about paving the way for a new and experimental hybridity.

The foreground of piano is followed by the guitar dropping to a baseline accompaniment, allowing for more fresh, digitalised sounds to emerge. This is ultimately about setting up an ontological displacement, which aligns itself nicely with the lyrics, 'I wonder who you'll fuck when I die / And if I tried to call, would you cry?'

Nevertheless, at around fifty-four seconds, an *undisturbing* occurs in the instrumental arrangement, which is followed by the pleasurable release of the drop itself. The guitar remains as a distortion, however, rising and falling across the beat, emerging and submerging when necessary.

The constituent elements are brought together by a satisfying, rhythmic percussion. One of the most satisfying elements of this track in particular originates in the subtle and nuanced utilisation of hi-hat patterns traditionally associated with the atmospheric synths of hip-hop subgenres. Taking atmospheric synths and placing them in the foreground to create a dreamy, hypnagogic soundscape represents the praxis of an aesthetic which seems to reach a commercial and accessible maturity in a track like '16 Lines'.

'Is anybody out there? (Is anybody out there?)' So much of contemporary criticism concerns liminal spaces and yet the echo here recalls a genuine liminality. 'Can anybody hear me? (Can anybody hear me?)', Peep sings with a profound retrospective dimension where the arrangement of motifs and lyrics develop at their most masterful.

– Sad Boy Aesthetics –

The synth at three-minutes-twenty-six-seconds is so unbelievably perfect, for example, building upon the cadence of the initial drop to form something extremely cathartic. Following this progression, however, the track collapses back into the comfortable resonance of an alternative rock vibe, signalling our return from a moment of emotional resonance.

(つ◕‿◕)つ

We also begin with guitars on Awful Things[88] featuring Lil Tracy. In many ways, this song is structured in a similar, albeit increasingly accessible way. It starts with the guitar and vocal progression, before moving towards a more commercially-aware experimental form, which feels acutely self-aware of its market position. I can't help but observe the prevailing 'business ontology' of the music industry in terms of the official music video for this track, especially.

Here, I think the fruition of Peep's experimentalism is accompanied (and largely restricted) by 1) the tried and tested mise en scène of an American high school as a space of juvenile delinquency and 2) the neon aesthetics as a form of visual sensemaking; this is all very edgy, look at how the walls glow in the dark, and so on...

I sometimes wonder if Lil Tracy's reluctance to be on this track stemmed from Peep's movement towards a more marketable image. The look of an awkward, high school loner, for example, that may or may not play emulated versions of 'Doom'. This is not to put the hurt on a track like 'Awful Things', but rather to highlight a distinction between an authentic vision and an artist at a thoroughly mediated and commercial apex.

(つ◕‿◕)つ

If 'Awful Things' represents the commercial apex, then a track like WitchBlades[89] – also featuring Lil Tracy – might come to represent the authentic vision in all its sad and conflicted glory.

(つ◕‿◕)つ

'I know that you want me, you know that I want you…' Lyrics such as these indicate a post-limerent state where two people have finally decided they want to fuck each other. What constitutes love in a world where love has already gone the way of the real? 'Feelings are never true.' Baudrillard writes, 'They play with their mirrors.'

In terms of lyrical narrative, intimacy is achieved on The Brightside[90] through a mutual appreciation of memory and self-reflection, 'I know that they haunt you too', Peep sings, specifying the relationship as one of melancholic facilitation. A certain 'paradisiacal' love can be found in the facilitation of 'ordained transgression', to use Slavoj Žižek's phrasing from 'Trouble in Paradise'[91].

'Just look at the Brightside,' Peep platitudes, a tinge of ironic distance, 'Just look at the club lights.' He concludes. One of the bodily cruelties of libidinous hedonism, risen through the predominance of the materialist ideology of our time, is convincing the mind that all it wants and needs from this world is physical intimacy without any such emotional affinity; 'This isn't what love's like…' Peep sings, 'That's for sure.'

(つ◕‿◕)つ

'You were the one, that's what I told myself / I don't even know myself / Or control my 'self' at all…' Peep sings with retrospection, offering a critique of his notions of an existent 'self' – and what that 'self' may come to desire. Here, love as melancholic facilitation crosses over into a track like i crash, u crash[92] featuring Lil Tracy. As a side note, one of my favourite YouTube versions of this song features an anime aesthetic taken from Hayao Miyazaki's 'Spirited Away'[93] (2001). There is something about great music that has the tendency to spirit you away to an elsewhere world where you are completely and totally understood as a human being.

(つ◕‿◕)つ

I always wanted to live in one of those houses in the suburbs with picket fences and a flamingo ornament in the lawn. I think about this when I listen to a song like Driveway[94] – and I don't know why. Perhaps these preoccupations emerge from the imagery of the song, 'I can't sleep and I can't eat / The same old shoes still on my feet / The same old grass still on my lawn / But it died since you've been gone...' There is something unexpectedly intimate and personal about the territory of driveways, the places we park our cars when we come and go, recurrent as ritual.

(つ◕‿◕)つ

'What was it? Just between us.' Ted Kaczynski (Paul Bettany) asks Jim Fitzgerald (Sam Worthington) in the 'Manhunt: Unabomber'[95] (2017) TV series. 'When did it all click?' There is a silence between them. Kaczynski continues. 'Well – for me – it all began in Chicago. One day this mockingbird began singing in the backyard there. You know that puffed up confidence, just belting out his song.' Kaczynski waves his hand like an opera singer. 'And I began to realize that the mockingbird was singing the car alarm.' He mimics the car alarm. 'You know the one?' He mimics it a second time. 'And I just sat there listening to that poor, dumb bird for maybe an hour straight, thinking – what have we done? ...how wrong that was. It stuck with me, I guess. I kept coming back to it. Just trying to figure out where in the world we had gone so wrong that it had ended up here.'

'For me it was the part about driving.' Fitzgerald tells Kaczynski. There is a long, sullen pause. Kaczynski leans forward; keen to hear more. 'Every time I got in the car, I thought about it. The more I drove, the more it made sense.' Fitzgerald considers his own words carefully. 'There was this one night where I was driving home from work and there was nobody on the street. I mean no body.' The scene cuts to Fitzgerald sitting in his car, late at night, the blanketed darkness broken only by the eerie gaze of street lights turned to red. 'I'm sitting at a red light, just waiting. Waiting.' He says, the light painting his skin the colours of a strip club interior. 'And there's no cars anywhere. Still, I sat there. I obeyed. That's when I realised, it's not about technology. It's not about machines. It's about what they're doing to us. *It's about what they're doing to us.* It's about what they're doing to our hearts, because our hearts are no longer free.'

'And you wanted to be free.' Kaczynski replies. 'You wanted your human dignity. Your autonomy. Everybody wants that.'

The criminal profiler scratches the table nervously, composes himself, looks up. Kaczynski delivers a hard truth. 'People want it so badly they're dying by the thousands everyday just trying to salvage some of their humanity.'

'Okay –'

'Think about this.' Ted interjects. 'More people have died from suicide in just the time we've been talking than I allegedly killed in my entire career. More people die from antidepressants. Plastic surgery. Fast food. Why is everyone so terrified of me?' He asks. 'And ask yourself this question, why are these men in suits so desperate to prove that I'm crazy? I will tell you. It's because they know that I'm right. I'm awake. They're asleep, and they're terrified that they might have to wake up too, and turn off their cell phones, and their TVs, and their video games, and face themselves the way that you and I have.'

A dialogue has always been the most beneficial way to face The Way I See Things[96] which also happens to be the name of a Lil Peep track whose unofficial upload to YouTube features yet another anime aesthetic; a still life, a blinking street light – *a red light* – a green 'walking man' in the rain. 'I'm clinically insane.' Peep sings on this track. 'Walkin' home alone, I see faces in the rain.'

Something could be said about the Foucaultian reading of insanity; madness as a construction of pure reason, an enlightenment reason that Herbert Marcuse would reveal as comedically paradoxical (dare I say, Kafkaesque). In the fourth video of the eight-part lecture series, 'The Self Under Siege: Philosophy in the Twentieth Century' (1993), Rick Roderick, speaking on Marcuse, says the following:

'...the crisis that was always at the heart of the enlightenment if you go back and look at it, the crisis that was always working on it was something like this. The attempt to demystify the world, the attempt to make the world, as it were, transparent to reason carried with it a strange dark side, always. And you may notice this when you watch television now. The more we, as it were, cleared the fields of the traditional religious views, the more that we became convinced that science – and one term for that Marcuse uses is "Instrumental reason"; reason used as an instrument for changing nature and human beings – the more that the enlightenment project progressed, it simply turned out not to be the case that we became less afraid in the face of the unknown. No, the unknown appeared more terrifying than ever, and it wasn't the case that we became less dogmatic, as a matter of fact, the sciences have now branched out into so many areas that the only way anyone could believe in any of them is dogmatically since none of us could study them because we don't have world enough or time.'

'Work is over, so it's time to go home.' Roderick continues, referring to the paradoxical nature of Marcuse's "Instrumental reason". 'It's rational to want to go home after work. On my view of the good reading of Marxism, that's the most rational thing we want all day; is to get away from work, it's very rational. So, each individual actor's decision to run out to their car and to get onto the freeway is rational. How about the outcome? Well the outcome is that everybody is sitting on the freeway breathing each other's smoke and sitting on their butt. The outcome is irrational! The outcome of a whole… see, there was no reason. Because the enlightenment focused upon reason as individuated, individual, atomic, they didn't see that the overall effects of reason working that way might themselves prove to be irrational.'[97]

Brad Pitt, playing an environmentalist with anti-corporatist fanaticisms in the 1995 film, 'Twelve Monkeys'[98], says, 'Very few of us here are actually mentally ill. I'm not saying you're not mentally ill, for all I know, you're crazy as a loon. But that's not why you're here. You're here because of the system. There's the television, it's all right there; look, listen, kneel, pray. We're not productive anymore, we don't make things anymore, it's all automated. What are we for, then? We're consumers. Buy a lot of stuff, you're a good citizen – but if you don't buy a lot of stuff, if you don't, what are you? What are you then, I ask you? – Mentally ill.'

Writing a foreword to a book, I once described myself as like Brad Pitt in the movie 'Twelve Monkeys' because of 1) how physically attractive I am 2) the schizomanic stylistic qualities appertaining to my critique of hyperreal systems, which is the only form of critique worth pursuing in a rhizomatic world. From the way I see things, (to use Lil Peep's lyricisms, here), there is, perhaps, nothing more hyperreal than the dichotomy of the rational and the irrational.

(つ◕‿◕)つ

I want to compare the Benz Truck in Benz Truck (гелик)[99] to the Benz Truck in Yung Lean and Bladee's 'Opium Dreams'[100]. (I assume this is also a Benz Truck, it sure looks like a Benz Truck; even so, both videos feature large, four-wheel drives. (I've since confirmed with my Mercedes-Benz driving buddies that it is, indeed, a Benz G-Class. (I still don't really know what that is – or how to differentiate between the various types of Mercedes-Benz.))) Even so, there is something ironic about the Benz Truck, a vehicle designed to reach otherwise inaccessible, rural spaces with relative ease, whose sign-value is happily being used by young people, here, who seem, at least, simultaneously unhappy (with the prevailing materialist dogmatisms of pseudo-secularism, perhaps), now seeking sanctuary in spaces we traditionally associate with the religious and the ritualistic; which is to also implicate themselves within the desire for something utterly transcendental.

An orthodox church, in the case of Peep's official music video, and the pagan iconography of circle casting, as observed in Yung Lean's video for 'Opium Dreams'. Despite the Baudrillardian sign-values of success and wealth traditionally associated with such expensive vehicles, there is something captured in both the lyrics for 'Benz Truck (гелик)' and 'Opium Dreams' which reveals the 'depressive hedonia' of social reality.

'Night of the soul, dark, dark', Bladee sings, a reference to the poem by Spanish mystic and poet, St. John of the Cross, which may or may not have been inadvertently taken from a number of reference points since its first conception in the sixteenth century. Initially, in terms of Roman Catholic spirituality, the phrase had come to refer, essentially, to a sense of spiritual crisis, which has since transcended the remits of Catholicism to refer more broadly, I claim, to the sense of existential dread that came to be described by Jean-Paul Sartre's Antoine Roquentin in 'La Nausée'[101]. 'Off the- off the next day,' Bladee sings in the first verse, 'dread, dread…' He repeats.

The juxtaposition of something pleasantly melodic with these dark lyricisms informs the aesthetic of such depressive hedonia. Nonetheless, 'Opium Dreams' is also a track largely concerned, especially in terms of the music video, with the aesthetics of spirituality and witchcraft; which have become

– Sad Boy Aesthetics –

frequent and reoccurring motifs across the sad boy aesthetic itself. (It should also be noted, the popularity of witchcraft (occultures) as a growing phenomenon, perhaps out of this Marcusian critique of "Instrumental reason" as providing no alleviations for a world that now seems more terrifying than ever.)

In 'Besom, Stang & Sword'[102], Christopher Orapello and Tara-Love Maguire write that 'outside the bounds of modern Neo-Paganism, witchcraft is not about *the* Goddess or *a* Goddess,' it is not concerned with the simple deification of nature, for example, but rather concerns notions of personal 'sovereignty', to use this term. For Orapello and Maguire, 'Witchcraft ties deeply into matters of personal governance and individual control.' Writing how these forms of spirituality 'addresses, with blood and sweat, the ills of life and society. In the hands of those who won't sit idle as life just happens to them, it's a tool for change. […] It's about living in the world, for better or worse. It is raw. It is dirty. It is a skillset, a discipline. It is an art. Witchcraft is dwelling in the woods where people rarely go. […] It is resting in forgotten caves and beneath silent trees.'

In 'Opium Dreams' we see Yung Lean and Bladee dwelling in the woods, casting circles beneath silent trees as a form of ritualised, personal sovereignty. From this analytical perspective, 'opium' and 'dreams' develop as metaphorical dissociations from 'the self', a music video that manifests as a Coleridgean vision in a dream: a fragment.

Slavoj Žižek's Hegelian reading of Christianity provides an interesting comparison to the use of Lean and Bladee's use of witchcraft as a form of personal 'sovereignty'. It may also offer an entry point into discussing the significance of the religious iconography found in the official music video for Peep's 'Benz Truck (гелик)'. In the following transcribed passage, Žižek asks us to consider reading *Christianity in a Pagan way*:

'[G. K.] Chesterton, my good Catholic theologian knew it, he says that moment, 'Eloi Eloi lama sabachthani' – God why have you forsaken me? It means this, how do you identify with God? Let's say I feel abandoned, God has left me, I'm in a Godless world – the Christian answer, again, is not 'Okay, let me pray hard, do good things, maybe I will re-establish contact [with God].' It's to say, but at that very point, when

I feel abandoned by God, I'm identified with Christ on the Cross who felt the same. That is to say, as Hegel puts it very precisely, I overcome the division from God by transposing it into God himself. This idea that my distance from God is inscribed into God himself. […] Intelligent theologians knew this. Even a conservative like Claudel – Paul Claudel – the great poet, he said, 'the ultimate mystery of Christianity is not that we are impotent without God but that God is impotent without us.' Okay, it gets more complex, but in this sense, I mean it quite literally, about being an Atheist Christian. I specifically don't mean all those simplistic ideas that Christianity can be realised in new Communist society, or whatever – all those dreams. No, I think that, again, the secret core of Christianity is precisely this acceptance of being on your own as a precisely divine gift.'[103]

In terms of this analysis, and how it may relate to the official music video, we can observe that when Peep isn't located at the exterior of a Christian Church, he can be found within its interior. Take, for example, the beginning of the track, where we also observe the vehicle – the Benz Truck, in this instance – travelling towards an undisclosed location, which we later find out to be the church itself, situated in an agrarian and rural setting.

The accompanying footage then features a montaging of stain-glass windows and altars, before landing on an image of Peep standing in front of a sign that says, 'ALL ALONE'. In terms of theism, make of that what you will; it seems when it comes to God, you are either with Hegel or Nietzsche, a very human, all too human dichotomy. *The interpretation is true.*

Nevertheless, despite everything written by Jacques Ellul, the paradoxes of technological society might allow the Benz G-Class as the machine that drives us towards a transcendent awakening; the genesis of which might first be observed in the spiritually evocative aesthetic choices of videos to tracks like 'Benz Truck (гелик)' and 'Opium Dreams'.

(つ◉‿◉)つ

> 'I found some Xanax in my bed / I took that shit, went back to sleep / They gon' miss me when I'm dead, I lay my head and rest in peace / I'm praying to the sky[104] and I don't even know why…'

– Sad Boy Aesthetics –

(っ◕‿◕)っ

Sometimes I stand in the mirror and try to mimic Marlon Brando from 'On The Waterfront'[105] (1954), sometimes I mimic George Bailey from 'It's a Wonderful Life'[106] (1946), and sometimes I even try to mimic Lil Peep's lyrical expressions in a track like Give U The Moon[107] which also features an audio sample of George speaking to Mary outside the abandoned house where they throw stones and make wishes in 'It's a Wonderful Life'.

'You want the moon?' George asks. 'Just say the word, and I'll throw a lasso around it and pull it down.'

Here's the thing, Mary doesn't want the moon, George; she just wants you to stay with her forever. 'To love someone is to isolate him from the world...' Jean Baudrillard writes; the world of prayers and wishes has always belonged to the world of fatal strategies.

(っ◕‿◕)っ

'At this point, it is perhaps worth introducing an elementary theoretical distinction from Lacanian psychoanalysis which Žižek has done so much to give contemporary currency: the difference between the Real and reality.' Mark Fisher writes in 'Capitalism and the Real' – the words printed here, found on page seventeen of 'Capitalist Realism'.

From a reading of Žižek and Alenka Zupancic, Fisher is keen to create a distinction between reality as the 'highest form of ideology', to quote Zupancic, the 'ideologically mediated' worldview and the 'The Real' in terms of its Lacanian definition.

'For Lacan,' Fisher continues page eighteen, 'the Real is what any 'reality' must suppress; indeed, reality constitutes itself through just this repression. The Real is an unrepresentable X, a traumatic void that can only be glimpsed in the fractures and inconsistencies in the field of apparent reality. So one strategy against capitalist realism could involve invoking the Real(s) underlying the reality that capitalism presents to us.'

What is Fisher proposing here – nihilism as a fatal strategy?

The irony of invoking 'The Real' is that one can only ever invoke the trauma of the void: the profound actualities of such emptiness. After all, as Fisher writes with total Baudrillardian awareness, the real is a traumatic void; a void as an absence – a liminal space – which is represented only by the volume of an entire desert. Nonetheless, within every reality there remains the spectral surplus of absences. This is where hauntology begins.

Ghosts represent the spectral surplus in a world that prioritizes material reality. A track like Lil Peep's Ghost Girl[108] represents a textbook example of Mark Fisher's 'downer haze' and both the thematically consistent iconography of ghosting, and ghosted love, found in similar tracks, alongside the spectral surplus of libidinal desires glimpsed through the 'fractures' of an 'apparent reality'.

'I know I need my own girl…' Peep sings, an epistemic loneliness alleviated temporarily by drugs and sex, and yet he remains haunted by this transgressive, libidinal desire for a ghost girl, a simulacrum. 'Love me for a night, girl, hate me in the mornin'/ Yeah, I know you're tight girl, so I make her blow me / Lil Peep…'

What other repressions are being explored, here, in these lyrics? Tragic, male fantasy – perhaps? More often than not, the ghost girl imagery, no less, ends up inside the solipsistic principalities of masturbatory and hedonistic fascinations. Perhaps, there are only ever two ways to escape this reality; masturbation and death. And there is nothing like the sick cohabitation of both. So much of human complication and salaciousness cannot be assimilated into the system; it must remain *accursed*.

'Yet environmental catastrophe features in late capitalist culture only as a kind of simulacra,' Fisher writes, 'its real implications for capitalism too traumatic to be assimilated into the system.' Wrong. One of the worst presumptions about capitalism is that it cares for its own survival; notions of survival and catastrophe are very human projections onto the nature of operative realities; 'And this is the victory of the other nihilism,'[109] Baudrillard writes, as providing a reality that conceals with veneer the nihilism of the system itself.

Fisher is guilty – as is so much Marxian critique – of this all too human presumption that operative realities should *and are* geared towards life over death. Realities are more complicit with the underpinning of a Freudian death drive than they are concerned with sustaining life. (Historically speaking, even religious reasoning, the reasoning that defined so much of human civilization, has associated existent life, the agency of life, as a preparatory tool for one's death, to take one example; it seems almost trite and platitudinal to mention this now, largely because it is both trite and platitudinal to mention religion in terms of its fascinations with death; life as temporary, death as eternal, blah, blah, blah.) Today, capitalism speaks through the words of the band 'Trooper' from 1977 – 'We're here for a good time not a long time.'[110] This is instrumentally reasoned. After all, science tells us what we are currently doing to the planet.

As a sad boy of the hyperreal order, a consequence pertaining to melancholia as its fundamental passion, I speak through Baudrillard's 'Simulacra and Simulation' only as a simulacrum of myself from which '… the system is summoned to answer through its own death[.]' Let them know 'I am a terrorist and nihilist in theory' even when 'such a sentiment is utopian. Because it would be beautiful to be a nihilist, if there were still a radicality – as it would be nice to be a terrorist…'

(っ◉‿◉)っ

The track U Said[111] provides the cohabitation of two songs juxtaposed. The preliminary guitars and vocals and pulpy hi-hats provide an accompaniment to the drop that occurs at around two minutes where the listener observes a tonal shift towards an entirely new sound. Peep moves away from the initial introspection of 'time and pain' towards another collective disclosure: 'Sometimes life gets fucked up (fucked up) / That's why we get fucked up (we get fucked up)'. In many ways, the song mimics the effects of manic intoxication, moving away from a pensive timbre to a sudden and exuberant sound, a repeating mantra, 'I can still feel your touch / I still do those same drugs…'

(っ◉‿◉)っ

'Now I'm looking for a ghost girl' Peep sings on Runaway[112], 'I ain't never gonna find her.' I don't want to run around the tree when it comes to the prevalent and obvious frequency in which Lil Peep uses the whole ghost girl imagery thing. I also don't want to use this track as an awkward segue into mentioning Maria again like I'm crushing on her or something creepy like that. I wouldn't want to give the wrong impression.

...

(つ◕‿◕)つ

'There are two art markets today.' Baudrillard writes on page-nineteen of 'The Transparency of Evil'[113]. 'One is still regulated by a hierarchy of values, even if these are already of a speculative kind. The other resembles nothing so much as floating and uncontrollable capital in the financial market: it is pure speculation, movement for movement's sake, with no apparent purpose other than to defy the law of value. [...] it is a kind of space opera in the hyperspace of value. Should we be scandalized? No. There is nothing immoral here. Just as present-day art is beyond beautiful and ugly, the market, for its part, is beyond good and evil.'

Drunk in a bar in China I once had a conversation in broken and awkward Mandarin with a guy who let me wear his gold chain necklace whilst I talked incessantly about wanting gold teeth like Lil Peep, and I'd sing the lyrics from Gym Class[114] – 'Lil Bo peep with a brand new flow too / Lookin at my teeth like you never seen a gold tooth / Never in the streets cause I never leave my home / If you wanna live a dream I ain't coming bitch I told you...'

That night I sobered up by walking around the city, feeding stray cats, and taking photographs of my favourite vending machines against a backdrop of neon lights; 'there is a loneliness in this world so great' Bukowski once wrote, 'that you can see it blinking in neon signs...'[115]

There is a hidden beauty in the construction and design of vending machines, which concerns Baudrillard's *materialization* of aesthetics; 'It is often said that the West's great undertaking is the commercialization of the whole world, the hitching of the fate of everything to the fate of the commodity.' Baudrillard writes in 'Transaesthetics', where the 'The great undertaking will turn out rather to have been the aestheticization of the whole world...'

'Trash has always served my dreams well', Hollings writes, 'that is to say, Trash has been the outer form, the material

– Sad Boy Aesthetics –

expression of my dreams: of tomorrow, of life in space, of the blissful alienation from this world that I have always craved.' Here, I claim Hollings' Trash Aesthetics can be conceptualised within Baudrillard's first market of speculations, where trash aesthetics remains as a manifestation concomitantly adhering to a system of values whilst complicit within a refusal to obey 'the good order of things' where trash 'can never be reformed or rehabilitated' and yet remains accustomed to hierarchical regulation. Here, trash plays with its mirrors; it relies on the referential nature of good, puritanical art. It is impossible to imagine the holy without its desecrated forms.

A track like 'Gym Class' also embodies Baudrillard's first market of aesthetics – still regulated by a hierarchy of speculative values – whilst simultaneously occupying this trashy refusal to obey convention, which is to also render transparent the spaces 'beyond beautiful and ugly [...] beyond good and evil.' A strange reading of Baudrillard, perhaps, but who cares, anyway? Nonetheless, 'Our images are like icons:' Baudrillard continues in 'Transaesthetics', 'they allow us to go on believing in art while eluding the question of its existence. So perhaps we ought to consider art solely from an anthropological standpoint, without reference to any aesthetic judgement whatsoever.'

Through the precession of simulacra, we have arrived at the landscape of e-girls and sad boys, the aesthetic values of our time transposed onto the ecstatic communications of the hyperreal, a thoroughly anthropological standpoint. *My reading* of the aesthetics discussed here should only be taken from this anthropological standpoint, there is no aesthetic judgement to be made beyond saying how our melancholia is today communicated in the spaces of transaesthetic output, as is our nihilism, and why shouldn't it be?

'Trash, by virtue of its boundless corruption and endless larval mutation,' Hollings writes, 'is the material embodiment of hope.' There is hope, but not for aesthetics. 'My project has always been about aesthetics rather than morality...' Hollings concludes, and yet morality always finds a way; even in speculative forms, which is the only morality available to us. Even so, present-day morality is, perhaps, concerned only in terms of its ability to exhibit itself as a virtue.

'Most present-day images,' on the other hand, 'be they video images, [...] audiovisual or synthesized images',

Baudrillard writes, 'are literally images in which there is nothing to see. They leave no trace, cast no shadow, and have no consequences. The only feeling one gets from such images is that behind each one there is something that has disappeared.'

Here, in reference to the official music video to Lil Peep's 'Gym Class', we can see how sad boy aesthetics captures the aesthetic transposition into the hyperreal as a profound act of disappearance. In the video, Peep points towards the liminal environment of the natural world; the wind that lifts the sand. 'Like all disappearing forms, art seeks to duplicate itself by means of simulation,' Baudrillard concludes, 'but it will nevertheless soon be gone, leaving behind an immense museum of artificial art…', or – perhaps – an immense, bright labyrinth, a swirling noise of meaningless and empty communications.

(つ◕‿◕)つ

Lil Peep's Beat It[116] builds upon the foundation of beautiful piano chops later accompanied by some of the softest hi-hats and rhythmic resonance produced on any track discussed here. It produces a haunting quality with the piano recalling the image of someone playing alone, unaccompanied on stage, performing within an empty theatre, hitting keys melodically, forming a half-remembered song of another time, long ago. It is in this process of disappearance that we might find beauty; *Mono no aware* – 物の哀れ, もののあはれ – ephemera.

'… all the world's insignificance has been transfigured by the aestheticizing process. It is often said that the West's great undertaking is the commercialization of the whole world, the hitching of the fate of everything to the fate of the commodity. The great undertaking will turn out rather to have been the aestheticization of the whole world…'

Jean Baudrillard, The Transparency of Evil

PART III: CONNECTIVE ANALYSIS:

Wittgenstein's Aesthetics and Baudrillard's Aestheticization

– Sad Boy Aes

(つ◕‿◕)つ   Alex

The following paragraph is taken from Professor Hagberg's Entry on 'Wittgenstein's Aesthetics', found in the 'Stanford Encyclopedia of Philosophy':

> '[Wittgenstein] is eager to show the significance of making connections in our perception and understanding of art works—connections between the style of a poet and that of a composer (e.g. Keller and Brahms), between one musical theme and another, between one expressive facial depiction and another, between one period of an artist's work and another. Such connections—we might, reviving a term from first-generation Wittgensteinians, refer to the kind of work undertaken to identify and articulate such connections as "connective analysis"— are, for Wittgenstein, at the heart of aesthetic experience and aesthetic contemplation.'[117]

In terms of 'connective analysis'[118] and its deft, investigative uses, we might begin with an exploration of the contemporary ballad form, and how it relates to the overall formulation of the sad boy aesthetic. Tracks such as Lil Peep's Veins[119] recalls to mind Joji's 'Ballads 1'[120], an album that combines the emotive melodies of piano with lo-fi and trip hop vibes.

You can find some beautiful piano on 'Veins', for example, a track that is simultaneously tragic and sad and pleasant to listen to, which also happens to encapsulate so much of these cultural products, connectively speaking, particularly in relation to invoking feelings of hedonistic melancholia, which should be regarded as the pinnacle element of aesthetic unification. (In relation to the aesthetics discussed, here, of course.) In terms of Joji's 'Ballads 1', look no further than the official video for 'YEAH RIGHT'[121], for example, as a pre-eminent example of hedonistic melancholia. Here, Joji sings:

> 'I'ma fuck up my life
> We gon' party all night
> She don't care if I die
> Yeah, right, yeah, right...'

In addition, Joji tracks such as 'SLOW DANCING IN THE DARK'[122] and 'WANTED U'[123] encompass additional themes of limerence and libidinal desire. That first song concerned with love's failure to materialise entirely, 'You looked at me like I was someone else...', he sings, a reality later finding its natural continuation in a song like 'TEST DRIVE'[124], where intimacy is explored, not in terms of love but in terms of a very transient, libidinal experience; 'She don't wanna tell lies / She just wanna feel alive...' This stands in direct contrast to what the protagonist really wants from a relationship, explored here, albeit metaphorically in the imagery of car driving; 'I'm looking for a long ride (Looking for a long ride) / She just want a test drive...'

Moreover, these tracks are concerned with frequent, borderline-ish fluctuations between melodramatic emotion and deadpan delivery with such dramatic oscillations seemingly inferred from psychiatric notions of dissociation. After all, these tracks – as is the case with all cultural products produced in the vein of such sad boy categorisations – have prevalent dissociative qualities. In almost every official music video for the tracks on 'Ballads 1', Joji is often observed with a deadpan expression, giving no visual cues as to how he is really feeling inside. Visual cues have become a poor form of communication, it seems; lost in the ecstasy of metastatic acceleration they become malformed, lacking all sense of transparency. Instead, we must listen to words carefully.

Nonetheless, from the pathetic fallacy of rain drops on windows, to the sand kicked up in a desert, emotion remains transposed onto a surrounding environment where territories are presented as either miserable or liminal or both. They operatively reflect some kind of dissociated perception; an inability to communicate oneself entirely. Even so, what's often observable in Joji's lyricisms and visual artistry is the state of a person after the emotion or event has taken place. An aesthetic performance of retrospections. These are songs and emotions that have figuratively (and sometimes quite literally) taken place *after the orgy*. This is both mysteriously seductive and symptomatically revealing. In Baudrillardian terms, dissociation is the coping mechanism of an over-stimulated mind; no wonder it informs at the aesthetic level in an over-stimulated world, which is to say, a world of ecstatic communication. This may also explain the nature of the speaker's frequent and pathological anhedonia.

'I've been waiting my whole life / To know I wanted you', Joji sings on 'WANTED U', encapsulating, once again, the

Sad Boy Aesthetics

limerent desires of the speaker. Limerence is desire without end. Its endless continuation explored in tracks like 'CAN'T GET OVER YOU'[125], featuring Clams Casino, where Joji sings:

> 'I can't get over you
> Can't get over you
> And before I die, I pray that
> I could be the one
> That I could be the one
> But I won't be no fun
> If I can't have you, no one can...'

There is an obvious, obsessional darkness here, at the heart of all *limerent desire*, that remains largely unexplored within the contemporary landscape of culture and music, especially. This is what makes sad boy aesthetics so distinctive; it makes transparent the problems of such pathologies by shining a light through their symptomatic occurrence. This is unique since much of our aesthetic output, existing as products of cultural production, are increasingly associated with ethics and proliferating a sense of (hyper)morality within realities where no such profound ethical values can ever exist or be made.

'In the aesthetic realm of today there is no longer any God to recognize his own.' Baudrillard writes. 'Or, to use a different metaphor, there is no gold standard of aesthetic judgement or pleasure.' The same can be said for ethics, of course. After all, as Wittgenstein states: 'Ethics and Aesthetics are one.' What are the lasting implications of an aesthetics *without morals*? An aesthetics that faces the absences at the heart of our modes of living? These are the aesthetics of a relative moral order, which is to say, a morality that exists as pure simulation.

'Tell me more, I got a box cutter with your name on it / Tell me more, I can't stay this long on the same topic / I don't know you, but would I fall in love with you?' Joji sings on 'CAN'T GET OVER YOU', providing the juxtaposition of violent imagery with warped notions of love; the destructive violence of limerence, and so on. Perhaps, this darkness is the shadow of a culture that cannot be assimilated by systems of hyper-morality that offers no respite or sense of transcendence or absolution – beyond the point of cultural materialization. Instead, within the remits of these aesthetics, the creative output of Joji, for example, such darkness is treated with deadpan humour, the smile that defaces the whole discourse.

It becomes, in so many ways, 'satire played out with a straight face', as Hollings writes, an 'act of confession' in which 'culture is retold as a joke...' Similar to Hollings' trash aesthetics, these cultural artefacts – the sad boy aesthetic itself – develops as 'a bourgeois nightmare' represented through the powerful gratification of acknowledgements, 'not so much deferred as denied to the point of becoming a tangible presence.' It is no wonder Joji today posts under the Instagram Handle: sushitrash.

'I thought I'd vocalize my troubles, but nobody will listen / I know I'm cryptic and I'm weird, that shit comes off as indifferent / I don't wanna die so young...' The lyrics on a track like 'ATTENTION'[126] – also dealing with similar themes of limerence, and a longing for the attentions of *the limerent subject* – which for the most part feature the minimalistic construction of two piano notes and bass, followed by an 8-bit soundscape drop on the line break for 'I don't wanna die so young / Got so much to do / I don't smile for the camera / Only smile for you.' One thing that strikes me about this song in particular is that captivating use of 8-bit melody, which in terms of its use within the aesthetic feels hauntologically positioned, designed to capture something of the past in thoroughly nostalgic terms. It is less about bringing the past into the future, but refers more broadly to evoking both an ephemeral awareness, the persistence of ghosts, and a certain cultural period[127] where digital and virtual worlds informed a generational ideal – a satisfaction with life – that was never delivered.

When you consider the audience demographic here, the age of Joji himself – only a year younger than I am – for example, there is a sense of collective experience of and for this failure of satisfaction, deferred in favour of the sepulchral and the melancholic. After all, so much of the lyrical composition on 'Ballads 1' is concerned with death, and premature death, in particular. 'I would die for you / Do or die for you / Suicide for you', Trippie Redd sings on Joji's 'R.I.P.'[128] There is almost no desire for life, not because life is painful, but because life comes as a series of subsequent disappointments and indifferences, it seems. There is an absence of satisfaction; a depression, a depressive ontology, an anhedonia. Even success and wealth,

– Sad Boy Aesthetics –

according to Joji's speakers is not amenable to feeling good. Similar to Lil Peep's music, we could assume these speakers reflect the feelings of Joji himself, or – at the very least – the persona of a man whose real name is George Miller.

'I'm rich, but my A/C broke…' Joji sings on 'NO FUN'[129], a song about indifference and futility. A song where the speaker acknowledges that his friends are no fun, 'They all left one by one', he tells us, and yet the speaker cannot find fun by himself. Moreover, what caused his friends to leave? Is it friends that are no fun, or is this actually the psychological projection of a melancholic sad boy onto a now entirely absent influence? Either way, fun is rendered impotent. Nonetheless, without the exterior stimulus of 'friends', loneliness is preferable, not in necessarily hedonistic terms, but in the total and complete indulgence of the melancholic and solipsistic expression: 'I don't have no more dreams', Joji sings, 'I drive around on my own / Feel dead, but I feel my bones.' The song is almost entirely an interrogation into the nature of having fun, and whether fun is even obtainable in a world where once you 'open up' your 'cover's blown…' The song is entirely self-aware of such confessionalism, the confession itself, according to Hollings, operating as a continuation of the crime. This is, perhaps, the other pinnacle element of aesthetic unification; the brutal self-awareness of the melancholic hedonism that is taking place; the confessional nature of art as a form of failed absolution. Even so, Joji knows he is 'cryptic' and 'weird' but wants us to know he is not 'indifferent'.

What is he then, if not sad?[130]

(つ◉⌣◉)つ

Continuing along the channels of connective analysis, we might investigate a track like Lil Peep's Five Degrees[131] whose earliest upload features yet another anime aesthetic. This time around, we see an animated accompaniment, a sheltered apartment corridor, rain falling, once again – as it always does in images such as these. The pathetic fallacy of liminal spaces features heavily in both anime and the other items connectively associated with the sad boy aesthetic.

Liminality, coming from the Latin term, 'līmen' translates as 'a threshold', which creates the sure dichotomy of actually existing realities and their simulacra. This is to say how liminal space: corridors, hallways, stairwells, hotel lobbies, elevators, car parks, reception areas, airport terminals, train platforms, and so on, justifies such an existence as the threshold between two or more opposing realities. What can be said about The Real these liminal spaces come to divide and segregate?

Absolutely nothing.

In terms of Baudrillardian analysis, it seems such profound realities do not exist. In their materialized and manufactured glory, liminal spaces become the only reality we can ever truly occupy with total confidence. It is profoundly hyperreal in the sense that it creates the illusion of such opposing realities as a means of paving the way for its own justification. In other words, through the reference to an exterior, or opposing reality, the liminal space becomes a self-sustaining simulation, the threshold hinting towards exterior elsewhere worlds which suggest something profoundly existent as standing in relation to its manufactured artifice.

Everything is artifice, even reality. *Liminal Validation* of exterior actuality is so deeply comforting to us, so soothing to our sense of ontological displacement, that we have come to seek the liminal divide at almost every turn. I can't help but feel like contemporary fascinations with liminal space is actually an obsession with the disappearance of the real. The more focus directed towards the liminal divide, the more hope to confirm the existence of some exterior reality. A truly ironic and fatal strategy.

This also accounts for the uncanniness of liminality, I claim, which comes to suggest something of existence whilst keeping The Real at arm's length. Liminal space is the world of sure systems, stressed-tested for our convenience. As such, it develops with a sense of the *undisturbing*. Which is to say, simultaneously comforting and disturbing since they both provide a *sense of actuality*, whilst also recalling its absence. Reductively speaking, this may also explain the phenomenon of uncanniness in postmodern societies as an inability to distinguish reality from a simulation of reality. An encounter with the real which is to say the absence of the real often manifests as a thoroughly supernatural occurrence. Dare I say, in terms of connective analysis, a dissociation?

Liminal territories, in addition, confirm the mythologies of our culture; providing the space where the ecstatic communication of objects and signs can occur uninterrupted, transposed onto a thoroughly artificial network. So prevalent in our lives today, it is no wonder these spaces inform the emergence of new aesthetic forms.

In the official music video for 'Sugar'[132], for example, we see Bladee walking down a corridor reminiscent of an urban underpass; a liminal space dissevered by the cold reality of fluorescent lamps. He approaches a grimy stairwell. 'I can't take the truth today / So tell me a fairy tale'. Following these lyrics, there is the obvious contrasting of the black and white footage of a desolate and bleak underpass with the sudden and prevalent colour saturation of the natural world, a pink hydrangea and such, the classical architecture of sculptured representations and ionic columns. Within the invocations of such distant and mythologised imagery, we have entered the heavenly principalities of Bladee's 'fairy tale' dream world.

'You don't want me, do you?' He sings, summoning the limerent subject, where these words, later recalled through an immensely intertextual appearance on 'Sailor Moon & Hennessey'[133], where Yung Lean would conclude, 'You say that you love me, I don't know if it's true / When I go to sleep all I ever see is you…' Reversals are made whereby the speaker becomes the object of limerent desire. What is the banality of limerence to the sublimity of reciprocated love? Perhaps, this song represents the continuation of dissociative wish fulfilment, a dream state, dream-reality; the symptomatic desire to escape the suffocating banalities of this world. What is beauty, the pleasant and aesthetic forms also, which is to say sublimity in addition, other than a glimpse of a world without the banal as its lens of mediation?

(つ◉⌣◉)つ

'Postmodernity is said to be a culture of fragmentary sensations, eclectic nostalgia, disposable simulacra, and promiscuous superficiality, in which the traditionally valued qualities of depth, coherence, meaning, originality, and authenticity are evacuated or dissolved amid the random swirl of empty signals.'

Following Jean Baudrillard's analysis of the postmodern condition, perhaps it would be amenable to comment on the metaphorical transposition of the physical Rolodex of numbers and names into the virtual Rolodex of personalities and identities (disposable simulacra) from which the individual can manifest as and when required. Today, I must look respectable, whereas tomorrow is my day off with which I will slob around the house. Professionalism and the 'professional identity' are about the correct regulation of such artificial selves, the ability to hear about Karen's cancerous growth at the water cooler, before closing the deal with your corporate sponsor.

Over the years, I have learnt to regulate my face from between the perfect transparency of a smile, to the deadpan expression of a human being who feels only profound and total indifference. In a single hour, I may be required to cycle through my entire remit of emotions and identities to the point where any and all such states are rendered entirely banal and meaningless. Through societies' absurd games, I come to feel a sickness growing inside of me. A very surface-dwelling sickness, a sickness in which many kill themselves just to disguise.

No wonder such modes of living produce the mixed state cohabitation of self-hatred and deprecation with an almost manic grandiosity of self; since no one can ever entirely compartmentalize such identities. In 'The Conspiracy Against the Human Race', Thomas Ligotti provides the following insight:

'Within the hierarchy of fabrications that compose our lives—families, countries, gods—the self incontestably ranks highest. Just below the self is the family, which has proven itself more durable than national or ethnic affiliations, with these in turn outranking god-figures for their staying power. So any progress toward the salvation of humankind will probably begin from the bottom—when our gods have been devalued to the status of refrigerator magnets or lawn ornaments. Following the death rattle of deities, it would appear that nations or ethnic communities are next in line for the boneyard. Only after fealty to countries, gods, and families has been shucked off can we even think about coming to grips with the least endangered of fabrications—the self.'[134]

One fabrication Ligotti fails to observe is the fabrication of his own reality, which is to say his all-consuming pessimism. There is an entitlement to pessimism which relegates existence to a product of stark deficiencies. Nonetheless, what better way to exhibit the fabrication, the total simulacra of our

– Sad Boy Aesthetics –

time than through the metaphor of the mediated self? This text existing as an investigation into the sad boy aesthetic is largely concerned with an artist whose identity consisted as a fractured double; which is to also reveal a thoroughly aestheticized set of identities. Nothing I write should be taken as a personal critique of Lil Peep or a shallow ad hominem, of course. I am only ever in love with Peep's honesty as a revealing force. An acknowledgement of such mixed state cohabitations, self-hatred and deprecation with an almost manic grandiosity should be taken as perfectly admirable. That is to say, Lil Peep occupies a world of personal acceptances from which we should all feel envious.

Such aesthetics, and the aestheticization of identity, (which is to also represent, in more capitalistic terms, 'personal branding') is a major player in the contemporary landscape of cultural production, especially. In terms of the music industry, such aestheticization is self-evident from the earliest progenitors such as Sting, to name one already mentioned here, (whilst alternatives might include Ziggy Stardust, Blondie, Freddie Mercury, Prince, and so on) and yet one thing that unifies this sad boy grouping of contemporary artists, in terms of the aesthetic discussed here is this hyper-awareness of such manufactured identities. Joji, Bladee, Yung Lean and Lil Peep, for example, are all alter egos *born from digital spaces.* There is perhaps no other place in existence that has come to represent the artifice of identity quite like the internet. Moreover, these artists are very much self-referential and self-intertextual; they exist as identities within their own forms of cultural production. As such, they are hyper-aware to the nature of such performances; they are, for all intents and purposes, hyperreal.

'The double' Baudrillard writes, 'is an imaginary figure, like the soul, the shadow or the mirror-image, which haunts the subject as his 'other', causing him to be himself while at the same time never seeming like himself. The double haunts the subject like a subtle death, but a death forever being conjured away.' What's significant about Lil Peep's artistry, all sad boy aesthetics, is this ability to conjure away death, thoughts of death and suicide, in quite literal terms, in the lyrical proclamation of their very existence. In terms of aesthetic unification, Lil Peep becomes as a connective tissue. Take these lyrics from 4 GOLD CHAINS[135], featuring Clams

Casino, for example:

> 'She's tryna find the words, I'm tryna find this girl
> But it's so dark, and I was under club lights
> Call me on my iPhone, I don't pick it up much
> I've been losin' friends, I don't feel right...
>
> Four gold chains, gave two to my brothers
> Fame bring pain, but the pain make money...'

At every turn, this is exactly what it feels like Gus is doing with his alter ego; placing the paradoxical feeling of worthlessness and grandiosity, the simultaneous existence of 'darkness' (absence) and 'club lights' (artifice) alongside a sense of limerent desire, 'I'm tryna find this girl', all developing towards a hedonistic melancholia where 'I don't feel right' sits within a compartmentalised identity which later became thoroughly materialised through the artistry; which is to also say, aestheticized. A world where 'Fame bring pain, but the pain make money...'

How much of this identity is real and how much are contrived is unimportant, however, since all that matters, in thoroughly symptomatic terms, is the inability to distinguish reality from its simulation. This is to say, any perceived state of divergence between the reality of performances and the reality of The Real has entirely diminished. The performance of what we might call reality is the only sure reality that we know to exist. This is where hyperreality begins. Hyperreality is the performance of the actual. The prevailing idea explored by both Fisher and Žižek, that we cannot imagine a world outside of global capitalism is the result of such spectacular performances. Capitalist (Hyper)Realism, for example, presents as an ontological actuality where any alternatives are rendered entirely fantastical since the alternatives will always find themselves at odds with the dominant reality. As such, there is an almost mathematical beauty to simulated realities; almost as if such arrangement is cosmically informed.

(つ◕‿◕)つ

Kurt Cobain's mythology is referenced, quite openly, on a track like cobain[136] featuring Lil Tracy. In this track, melancholia has evaporated, replaced by the swirl of empty signals and identities.

I like to interpret Lil Tracy's lyricism here as a Baudrillardian critique of sign-values where the most a person can do to form an identity is mix 'American Eagle with some Ralph Lauren'. Nevertheless, in terms of an intertextual use of identities and values, I want to talk briefly about Kurt Cobain as an early progenitor of the melancholic disposition, particularly in relation to melancholia and its aestheticization within the culture.

At this point, the logical conclusion for many readers will be that sadness, limerence, desire, and so on, have always presented themselves on the thematic landscape of art and culture. An exploration of these themes in art and music, for example, is nothing new, of course. However, the primary connectivity of aesthetic unification, in relation to the sad boy aesthetic, especially, is the cohabitation of paradoxical signals; the cohabitation of the melancholic with the hedonistic, for example.

In many ways, we should perceive Morrisey as more 'Sad Boy' than Cobain since Morrisey actually presents an image of narcissism[137] alongside his image of melancholia. Within 'The Smiths', for example, there is the cohabitation of opposites taking place; self-loathing as a form of self-love. Take the lyrics from the track, 'I Know It's Over'[138], for example, with connective analysis in mind:

> 'And you even spoke to me, and said:
> "If you're so funny
> Then why are you on your own tonight?
> And if you're so clever
> Then why are you on your own tonight?
> If you're so very entertaining
> Then why are you on your own tonight?
> If you're so very good-looking
> Why do you sleep alone tonight?
> I know...
> 'Cause tonight is just like any other night
> That's why you're on your own tonight
> With your triumphs and your charms
> While they're in each other's arms..."

Limerent conclusions aside, a spectral narcissism of the 'so funny' and 'so clever' and the 'so very good-looking' hangs over the lyricism, pronouncing a world where I am not necessarily unlovable, but rather there is just not enough love in this world to love the person that I am with all my 'triumphs' and my 'charms'. If only people were better, Morrissey proclaims, then maybe I'd be happy.

Through this alternate perspective, 'Last night I dreamt that somebody loved me'[139], seems less about the deficiencies of the speaker, and more about the deficiencies of any potential lovers, who are always dumb and happy, always somewhere else, in someone else's arms, who remains equally as dumb and equally as happy. Perhaps this impression of 'The Smiths' adequately explains why so many listeners find Morrissey so detestable since he is, in every paradoxical way, infatuated with himself at the most juvenile level with such piteous honesty informing the point of aestheticization. Even so, Morrissey is hyper-aware to the performance of the melancholic disposition as a rudimentary paradox. Such heightened awareness becomes an aesthetic commencement. An indifference to the paradox.

There is, in addition, a performative element to Nirvana's melancholy also, which seems intricately tied to the hermeticism of their lyrics and resonance. 'He's the one / Who likes all our pretty songs / And he likes to sing along / And he likes to shoot his gun / But he knows not what it means…' Cobain sings on 'In Bloom'[140], a song and official music video almost entirely dedicated to the vapidity of the band's commercial image as an empty signifier of opposites.[141]

Even so, Kurt Cobain came to represent this 'Otherness', an anhedonia, perhaps, that could be assimilated into the ecstatic communication of the American consciousness, especially. Cobain was reduced to the state of an image, after all; which is to also say, aestheticized. Watching the 'Live On MTV Unplugged, 1993'[142] performance of Nirvana is enough to make me feel uneasy. One of the creepiest elements of watching Cobain perform in retrospect is not so much the performance of the band itself, but the performances of those around him, the facilitative nature of the crowd, and so on, who seemed to revel in the projection of Cobain's misery. Like all good icons, Kurt Cobain acted as a mirroring identity.

'Call me Cobain', Lil Peep sings, mirroring such performative capacities, the ability to transpose the signals of an entire culture onto a living and breathing agent of aestheticization, which is to say, exactly what Lil Peep

– Sad Boy Aesthetics –

achieved as an alter ego.

In 'Capitalist Realism', Fisher writes how "Alternative' and 'independent' don't designate something outside mainstream culture; rather, they are styles, in fact the dominant styles, within the mainstream. No-one embodied (and struggled with) this deadlock more than Kurt Cobain and Nirvana. In his dreadful lassitude and objectless rage, Cobain seemed to give wearied voice to the despondency of the generation that had come after history, whose every move was anticipated, tracked, bought and sold before it had ever happened.'

This is another expression of the Baudrillardian aestheticization at a cultural altitude. 'Cobain knew that he was just another piece of spectacle,' Fisher continues, 'that nothing runs better on MTV than a protest against MTV; knew that his every move was a cliché scripted in advance, knew that even realizing it is a cliché.' Fisher characterised this as a cultural paralysation, 'the one that Jameson described: like postmodern culture in general, Cobain found himself in 'a world in which stylistic innovation is no longer possible, [where] all that is left is to imitate dead styles, to speak through the masks and with the voices of the styles in the imaginary museum'. Here, even success meant failure, since to succeed would only mean that you were the new meat on which the system could feed.'

A similar analysis of the political dimension would be discussed in the interview, 'Things Surpass Themselves'[143]. In this interview with Florian Rötzer, Baudrillard would state: 'We know that every critique, every opposing force, only feeds the system.' Through a Landian-Bataillean Grotesquery[144], the system is, once again, characterised as an entity that must feed – and must be fed.[145]

(つ◉‿◉)つ

In the official music video to Nothing To U[146] we observe Lil Peep standing within a pentagram, complete with all the iconography of spellcasting, which is not so dissimilar to the images and accompaniments found throughout Yung Lean's album, 'Starz', for example – or to offer a more tenuous link, Bladee's album, 'Red Light'.

'"Sometimes you can be cruel and evil," you tell me / Put me in a spell' Lean sings on 'Put Me in a Spell'[147], which is accompanied by piano and the dreamy and hypnagogic beats produced by whitearmor. This is not to indicate, in any way, that such albums exist as products of Peep's influence, but rather to mention the obvious and significant influence of occultism and occultures over all these works, which is to also offer another point of aesthetic unification.

There is something about the imagery of occultism that fractures reality, of course, existing at the peripheral edges of instrumental reason. Within the pages of 'Besom, Stang & Sword', the authors discuss such magickal performance in terms of its ability to 'open people up to an undeniable facet of the human experience.' Witchcraft, according to Orapello and Maguire, 'challenges and reveals aspects of human consciousness and reality, it shows that there is indeed much more to the world than what's visible to the ordinary eye.'

The character of spirituality and witchcraft involves the dissolution process between the dividing forces that exist between the conscious and subconscious; one reality and another, as is the case with divination. Moreover, whilst 'Magick' is largely concerned with the projection of individual intent onto the cosmos, an affirmation of the potencies of individual and collective will in truly Nietzschean capacities, in addition, there comes with witchcraft a dissolution of psychologically entrenched dichotomies; especially when the formulation of such artificial (and often authoritarian) dogmatisms become inherently attached to societal indoctrination.

'If the ultimate goal of the study and practice of witchcraft could ever be expressed,' Orapello and Maguire write, 'it might include elements like testing the limits of your own reality…' There is an obvious and straightforward acknowledgement from the practitioners of witchcraft that holds the artifice of reality to account. Here, the world exists only as a sacred space without pathways, a world of seemingly manifested realities.

(つ◕‿◕)つ

> '...it seemed as though the entire day was coloured by the gloom, the irritability, the uneasiness, the nihilism that belonged to youth.'

> The Temple of the Golden Pavilion, *Yukio Mishima*[148]

White Wine[149] begins with chords of sepulchral magnificence maintained across the track by hi-hats and deep reverberations. It is a profoundly minimalistic composition where an acapella bridge later informs a drop towards the end of the track where Peep sings, 'Lord why, Lord why do I gotta wake up? / More wine, more wine, baby pour another cup...'

References to a religious significance by both Peep and Tracy within the song aids the facilitation of a sepulchral thematic positioning. An interesting piece of trivia recalls the track initially being titled 'Red Wine', which would, in addition, condemn the communal glass – red wine with all its ritualistic significance – to a dimension of maenadian chaos. The track is, however, more sepulchral than anything else. The term used here to describe the imagery of *ritualized death* and interment that manifest across the track. 'I'ma get a Maserati just to take my life inside', Tracy speaks with cold indifference on a verse laced with the suicidal evocations of a glistening wrist.

Moreover, the track represents the culturalization of a deadening high, 'Took her to the crib and I show her how I die (how I die) / Every night, then I wake up and I'm still fuckin' high (I'm still high, yeah)' an intoxication that aids the sign of such obvious and troubled indifferences towards both life and death. '...inasmuch as we have access to neither the beautiful nor the ugly, and are incapable of judging, we are condemned to indifference.' Baudrillard writes. 'Beyond this indifference, however, another kind of fascination emerges, a fascination which replaces aesthetic pleasure.'

What replaces aesthetic pleasure, here? Answers are achieved, perhaps, within the personification of cocaine as 'a white bitch', 'hopped up in my ride' which later finds parallels with Lil Tracy's verse, the ecstasy of 'hoppin' out the Uber on a Friday' presumably to begin a weekend of hedonistic excesses. One thing that fascinates me about Lil Tracy's verse in particular is its continued and exact considerations of the aesthetics of Gothicism, the general mood of entropic diminishment that accompanies the lyricisms of the 'so magical'.

The verse features the sexy and transgressive landscape of 'castles' and 'Gothic' bitches. What is Gothicism but the general aestheticization of a certain atmosphere, place and period. A hyperreal atmosphere, no less, that has today informed our perception of castles as mysterious places full of lost and forgotten things; tangible principalities where history and mythology collide. So much of Lil Tracy's lyricism represents this world where Gothicism is transposed onto contemporary landscapes like a Gore Verbinski film.

Verbinski's 'The Ring' (2002), for example, is a beautifully shot film that concerns the wish fulfillment of technology and entertainment, with all the dreams of photorealism, as an accelerative towards death, and the death drive. Parallels can be drawn between the technological perceptions of Samara's cursed videotape and Lil Tracy's conception of a 'Maserati' as a Gothically insidious instrument of death existing within the contemporary landscape.

Both Verbinski's 'Pirates of the Caribbean: The Curse of the Black Pearl'[150] (2003) and 'A Cure for Wellness'[151] (2016) are, in addition, Gothic fairytales retold (or at least retold through the simulation of a retelling) for contemporary audiences. There is absolutely nothing about the 'Pirates of the Caribbean' franchise that renders any historical account of pirates. In fact, that first installment is almost entirely concerned with an immensely hyperreal account of undead buccaneers and British colonialism. 'Pirates of the Caribbean: The Curse of the Black Pearl' becomes the simultaneous juxtaposition of history with mythology, a dissolution of the dichotomy, which is to also say, a more truthful account of any actually existing reality. There is an honesty to such fictions since to acknowledge something as comically fictitious is to also acknowledge the erasure of what was once terrifying and true.

One thing that concerns Verbinski's films is this state of reality disintegration, the unfixed boundaries between real and artifice, between dreams and waking life, between hallucinations, fantasies, and elsewhere worlds. Between the ghost inside the television screen, and its encroachment into your living room.

– Sad Boy Aesthetics –

Following Lil Tracy's lyrics as an interrogation into the genuineness of love and its portrayed simulacra, 'She said she love me, she don't even know my real name,' there becomes something grotesquely Frankensteinian about sign-values, in addition, the Lovecraftian cohabitation of this Gothic bitch's 'love' within this system of objects; a Lilith of chaos stepping out of an 'Uber', brandishing a 'Gucci bag', high on 'cocaine'. Surely, these are gothic visions transposed onto contemporary forms, rendered through cold indifference, the indifference of acquired banality, perhaps, where the speaker asks, 'Lord why, Lord why, do I wanna die?'

'There is nothing immoral here.' Of course, as Baudrillard writes in regards to the aesthetics of our culture. In many ways, a track like 'White Wine' pertains only to the final seduction of numbing sensations, alcohol and cocaine, for example; the aestheticization of the death drive, self-destruction as a fatal strategy whereby nihilism is perhaps reconciled as an ideal form.

It is only at the very end of Yukio Mishima's 'The Temple of the Golden Pavilion', for example, where the protagonist considers the profound beauty of his nihilism, not as a source of mere and mindless destruction, but as the staging force for life's sublimity; an aesthetics of perfect ephemerality.[152]

(つ◉‿◉)つ

Acoustic guitars feature on the intro of OMFG[153] where we are told by a booming, masculine voice that 'this is a certified hood classic', before hi-hats are brought in, building towards a hyped-up accompaniment, a progression towards Peep's vocals.

The penetrating reverberation on the guitar strings, such fine-tuned and deep foregrounding recalls the emo symphonic of math rock and shoegaze. Initially, I feel positioned in the familiar topography of emotive music which stands in stark contrast to the sudden hybridity, an announcement of this 'certified hood classic' which recalls digitally disseminated forms of trap music. The pronouncement also foreshadows the hi-hat patterns that slap with a powerful proximity to the stringed instruments.

The blending of these genres within a cohabitational composition produces the disintegration and diminution of their exact geographical origins whilst emphasising their cultural impact in much broader terms. Nonetheless, the unique blend of dream pop and alternative rock with a rap inspired lyrical delivery is performed with masterful inflection and nuance.

The warming sensation of guitars, for example, invites us into the composition, providing a comforting nostalgia for those who grew up in the shade of the Southern California punk scene. These are the guitars of a miss you Blink-182 recalling the sad otherness found within popular punk; a sound that later acknowledged the defeats and downturns of a Post-9/11 world.

One thing that I love about Lil Peep's music is the way it seems to recall a cultural period as if looking at the present through a prophetic lens of retrospections. It feels like an amalgamation of tiny insignificances, the way scratches on vinyl and bygone sound samples are now sought after as a means of xeroxing a cultural period.

Culture is created through the xeroxing of this radical other. Yet, as with art, a copy is never entirely the original, the absence of the original's peculiarities, the hairlines of a painter's brush and so on are never entirely replicable. As such, rather than replicate the original, it could be argued that copies create entirely new forms. In many ways, a copy is reproduced only through a series of minor absences. Just as the original can be traced through its series of distinguishing characteristics, as does the copy retain elements of its own telling.

As such, Lil Peep's artistry is about genre retelling; a xerox as the aestheticization of these genres towards an amalgamation of new forms; a hybridity that separates the divide of differences towards the collective experience of the melancholic. Alongside additional experiences of such inescapable and immutable pain, this young man, at the level of the individual, at least, emerged from beneath a virulent culture recounting his identity through its process of aestheticization: 'I used to wanna kill myself', he sings, 'Came up, still wanna kill myself…'

(っ◉‿◉)っ

– Sad Boy Aesthetics –

Lil Peep's Lie To Me[154] acknowledges the predilection towards deception, our desire to be faced with the comforting untruths rather than any semblance of a potential actuality: 'Tell me you love me even if you lie to me / Tell me I'm ugly even if you vibin' with me…'

This stands in contrast with the demands of Bladee's 'That Thing You Do'[155], where the artist sings: 'Give me something, please, give me what I need / Show me something real…' Nonetheless, what really interests me about Bladee's album in particular, is the similar coalescence of traditionally associated dichotomies, depression and mania, to give the obvious example found as the unifying force par excellence.

Such simultaneous cohabitations are achieved throughout an album like 'Red Light' which drips with the similar gallows' humourism of Peep, Lean and Joji, in addition:

> 'Heard you say you wanna die, so do I
> Just do it like Nike, eat the night
> Heard you said you wanna play, then it's Fisher Price
> Your shoes faker than my smile, not surprised…'[156]

(つ◉‿◉)つ

In an interview published over a decade ago, Greg Drudy from Level Plane told 'Delusions of Adequacy' he hoped his label would still be putting out records in ten years' time. These days, the label's official website doesn't even exist anymore, and neither does Level Plane. If you check out their homepage, the links provided will send you to discounted rice cookers, or maybe even thousand-watt pump espresso coffee machines in black or, I don't know, puce and beige? Either way, it's not music.

When asked how Level Plane got started, Greg seemed to give an honest and rather brazen response, telling the journalist, 'One night we were assembling copies of the Saetia 7" and I was also looking through the current issue of National Geographic. An author was discussing photography and the need for a level plane. It seemed like an interesting phrase and we were at a loss for anything else at the time." I like to imagine Greg began shipping those copies of Saetia from the same dimly-lit basement in New York City.

Saetia was a band formed in that same city back in 1997. This was the year David Bowie performed his 50th birthday concert at Madison Square Garden before receiving his star on the Hollywood Walk of Fame. These late nineties' screamo bands were certainly not influenced by the pop sound of David Bowie; their influences were far more esoteric and subversive. Saetia's lyrical influences derived from mythology and religion, with the band's name referring to a brooding musical composition found on Miles Davis' 'Sketches of Spain'[157] where the religious tradition of flamenco music plays dominance. The technical influences of Davis' jazz music are there too, with Saetia's softer, melodic hesitations providing a standing ovation to the genre's historical innovation. Parallels continue with their instrumentals sounding invocative of personal difficulty; the modus operandi of blues music with its shouts and clamour. This is, I suppose, the heart and soul of their brand of screamo, played out to the point where it has found caricature in the cultural mainstream.

Somewhere online, there's a quote about skramz provided by Jeff Mitchell of Iowa State Daily, who wrote: "there is no set definition of what [this] screamo sounds like but screaming over once deafeningly loud rocking noise and suddenly quiet, melodic guitar lines is a theme commonly affiliated with the genre."

This is, of course, a simplification of the skramz genre, but a great simplification nonetheless. Whilst the initially jarring and often repellent nature of this sound found little, if any, commercial success, the influence of these bands reigns supreme across contemporary genres like 'Emo Rap'.

Essentially, skramz was a categorical term used to separate the screamo music of the late nineties with the mainstream screamo of today, although the vagueness and sincere validity of the genre continues to be a topic for debate. Aside from Saetia, examples of skramz can be found in bands like Orchid[158], Pg. 99[159], and arguably, more experimental bands like Circle Takes the Square[160]. Released in the same year as Saetia's formation, I Hate Myself's 1997's song, 'Caught In A Flood With The Captain Of the Cheerleading Squad'[161] is a good example of the soft/loud dynamic utilized by the genre.

In a sad turn of events, Level Plane ceased to exist in 2009. Today, the legacy of Greg Drudy's label continues through the support of a cult following. Within this community, most fans extend their listening habits to the other bands associated with the skramz genre. Fortunately, they'll never forget where

— Sad Boy Aesthetics —

Level Plane started. In a basement in New York City; Greg's National Geographic laid out between coffee cups and an ashtray of half-smoked cigarettes.

One morning when I was dying from pneumonia, before being admitted to the hospital that saved my life, I listened to both Saetia's album 'A Retrospective'[162] and American Football's 'LP1'[163] which is also considered a major influence on the 'Emo Rap' genre. 'LP1' renders perfect and clean guitars, coming and going, piercing the sombre atmosphere of French horns and vocal dysphoria.

Another album I listened to that morning, over and over again, was Radiohead's 'OK Computer'[164]. There is such a world-weary bitterness on tracks like 'Climbing Up the Walls'[165], 'And if you get too far inside / You'll only see my reflection', Thom Yorke sings over percussion and melodies that would later feature as a sample on Lil Peep's Falling 4 Me[166].

'OK Computer' represented a move away from the more rock-orientated and direct melancholy of 'The Bends', towards an emotional resonance that seemed far more categorically complicated. In many ways, 'OK Computer' shaped the creative culture of alternative music in mainstream terms, at least, coming to represent an album of genre recreations, Miles Davis meets electronica, for example, where compositions would flip between the dejected and the maniacal, observable on a track like 'Karma Police'[167], with all its melodic resonances, the hauntingly pleasant crescendo of, 'For a minute there / I lost myself, I lost myself.'

'OK Computer' came together through a series of failed representations made commercially viable. The inability for the naturalisation of jazz, blues and rock to ever authentically re-occur within the paranoid fakery of augmented landscapes and ecstatic communications: 'He buzzes like a fridge', Yorke sings, 'He's like a detuned radio.'

'OK Computer' came to represent the cross-cultural hybridity of genre splicing as a means of producing new entities entirely, which is to say the aestheticization of those failed recreations, particularly in regards to the emulated relationship between a particular genre and the culture that produces it. As such, a band like Radiohead presents as the most likely progenitor for the experimentalism in alternative rock that came to influence an artist like Lil Peep. Nonetheless, if 'OK Computer' was about anticipating a certain millennial attitude as a distant, intellectual conception, then 'Hellboy' was about that attitude's embodiment in very visceral terms.

In my early-twenties, I would bike three miles to my minimum wage job where I would conduct the banking procedures for a small business. Every evening, on my way back from the bank, I would walk past the coffee shop where I would watch Thom Yorke, the lead singer of Radiohead, working on his MacBook Pro, and I would watch Thom Yorke every day, and I would check on him – like he knew me too – and I'd wonder what he was up to when he wasn't there, every day, watching him drink a latte through the window or whatever.

I would think about Thom Yorke a whole lot, at that time, and I would alter my pace from a brisk walk to a light meandering, and I would stare through the window, and sometimes he would look up, like this one time he looked right at me, and I thought, "Thom Yorke just looked at me", and I hurried on, expressionless, knowing that it would be important to tell someone, one day, about my sudden and urgent interaction with Thom Yorke from Radiohead – how our eyes met, briefly, and so on, like in the time it takes for an autumn leaf to hit the ground.

Except, there was nobody in my life to tell, largely because I was always profoundly and completely alone with myself, and when such a memory was recalled, for example, as it is here, or like, I don't know, when someone who I was even mildly attracted to mentioned anything remotely related to Radiohead, even in passing, I would tell them this exact story, ostentatious in my expression, in fact, about working for a small business, conducting banking procedures every day, and walking past the coffee shop window where "this one time Thom Yorke from Radiohead really looked right through me."

Sad Boy Aesthetics

'The World and Life are one. …Ethics and Aesthetics are one.'

Ludwig Wittgenstein

PART IV: EPILOGUE:

Dreams & Disappearances

(っ◔ᴗ◔)っ

'And perhaps several people remember,' Nietzsche recalls, 'amid the dangers and terrors of a dream, successfully cheering themselves up by shouting: "It is a dream! I want to dream it some more!"

'Even the philosophical man has the presentiment that this reality in which we live and have our being is an illusion,' Nietzsche writes in 'The Birth of Tragedy', 'that under it lies hidden a second quite different reality.'

If Baudrillard is presumed correct, even momentarily, then this second reality has dissipated entirely, not with the sudden and abrupt flick of a light's switch, but with the gradual decreasing of the carrier signal by way of a soundboard's fader. This disintegration of reality has been captured in the Borges' fable, and only the promises of the simulation can take its place. 'Something has disappeared:' Baudrillard writes, 'the sovereign difference…'

Nietzsche's work is founded on the promises of this alternative reality, a sovereign difference, a reality of the human and the Dionysian, which has long deserted itself, deterred in favour of the melancholic and the virtual – a world of thoroughly transhuman networks.[168] '…everything miraculous has disappeared…' Wittgenstein states. Perhaps, there remains in our world today no divine forms of aesthetic expression, nor any such deliverance.

(っ◔ᴗ◔)っ

Nietzsche provides an interpretation of Schopenhauer, who thought, according to Nietzsche, that 'the trademark of philosophical talent' was 'the ability to recognize at certain times that human beings and all things are mere phantoms or dream pictures.'

For hyperreality, there are no certain times, the dichotomy of reality and simulation is always phantasmatic. Even so, an awareness of this hyperreal order is useless, it provides nothing in a world that provides nothing, as does the awareness of one's dreams in becoming a combative measure against a long night of terror. What good is the knowledge of water in a desert without any?

– Alex Mazey –

An absence of this profound actuality must inform the aesthetics explored within this text. Nonetheless, the dream *feels real,* doesn't it – and an awareness of the dream does not prevent us from living and suffering in the midst of its scenes.

(つ◉‿◉)つ

I once watched a documentary on the career of Stanley Kubrick where a cinematographer – I remember incorrectly, but it sounds about right – discussed his spiritual awakening upon watching '2001: A Space Odyssey'[169] (1968). Wanting to encourage my own spiritual awakening, I proceeded to watch all of Stanley Kubrick's films, from '2001: A Space Odyssey' to 'The Shining'[170] (1980), night after night, when eventually, through this perfect and sublime moment of providence, felt absolutely nothing whatsoever; only indifference.

Maybe, this was the point?

In the essay, 'Kubrick as Cold Rationalist'[171], Mark Fisher writes the following:

> 'Kubrick is no Romantic: he does not buy into the overprivileging of the subjective and the emotional. Nor is he, in any sense, a humanist: human beings are not at the centre of his cosmos, and his account of humanity is, to say the least, not positive. [...] But concluding that his rejection of these doctrines makes him a cynic, a nihilist or a remote modernist is to be misled by the humanism and Romanticism his work so effectively challenges.'

I managed to stay awake to 'Eyes Wide Shut'[172] (1999) after taking benzodiazepines (prescribed), discussing it afterwards, later having absolutely no recollection of the film whatsoever. I also watched the anime adaptation of Osamu Tezuka's manga, 'Metropolis'[173] (2001) after taking sleeping pills, where I also tried garlic mayo for the first time with fried potatoes or whatever and allegedly enjoyed it so immensely, asking everyone "where garlic mayo had been all my life?" I don't remember any of this, either. The best film to watch on sleeping pills is David Lynch's 'Dune'[174] (1984), however, which remains an underappreciated masterpiece; so bad it's good.

I recently watched Ari Aster's 'Midsommar'[175] (2019). Aster's two films 'Hereditary'[176] (2018) and 'Midsommar' are so profoundly disturbing for no other reason than how they come to represent the wish fulfilment of a generation who subconsciously desire a spiritually-realised ideological conviction and the dissolution of atomic individualisation towards a collective and predetermined destiny. This is no better represented than in the smile of the May Queen herself, who comes to find solace in her fate, a fate that frees her from the cold emptiness of America. Sad Boy Aesthetics is concerned not with the realisation of such fulfilments, but with their complete and total absence.

What's disturbing is Aster's cold rationality juxtaposed with an equally cold oc-cult-ism. There is a Kubrickian element to such filmmaking, an aesthetic which says absolutely nothing about morality, whilst simultaneously revealing the paradoxes of any such ethical distinctions. It forces us to view all modes of living, all such convictions, through the prism of their justifications. A heightened consciousness becomes dangerous territory for a mind that seeks conviction without justification. I am so painfully platitudinal, here.

What I should be writing is something really presumptuous; consciousness operating less as an aberration and more as a source of regulation. As the cosmos is structured towards sustaining life, consciousness brings balance as a force geared towards sustaining death. Inasmuch there is so much talk about the universe's great potency for life, and very little discussion on its proclivity towards ending it.[177]

Aster's two films reveal, in addition, the pinnacle element of human desire as outsourced responsibility; the desire to succumb to one's fate, no matter how gruesome or evil that fate may have once appeared. These films are ultimately concerned with human agency, our hatred of the existential endowment, and the subsequent thirst for annihilation we have now come to exhibit as a species.

'Kubrick is no emotional pornographer - the point is not to identify with the characters.' Fisher observes in his essay on Kubrick. 'Such identification would merely reproduce the redundant subjective narcissism upon which consumer culture runs. *What if the point were to escape from this hall of mirrors?*' Fisher asks, offering a forewarning to the aesthetics explored in this text. 'To see ourselves in these characters, yes, but from outside, instead of from inside, so that we appear not now as passionate subjects but mannequins trapped within the hideous, remorseless machines that produce and feed upon our *subjective intimacies*.' (Emphasis added). What is limerence and libidinal desire if not subjective intimacy? This is where Capitalist (Hyper)Realism begins, perhaps, as a hideous, remorseless machine; an aestheticization of the whole world and its intimacies.

'It is precisely Kubrick's coldness and slowness that are missed in a contemporary culture that is so obsessively 'warm' and 'fast'; ingratiating, emotionally exploitative, relentlessly fidgety. Kubrick took us out of ourselves: not via the transports of *ecstatic* fervour,' Fisher's words, here, emphasis added, 'but through the icy contemplation of what drives and traps us, and the vision of a universe indifferent to our passions. To see the mechanical deathliness of the human world from the perspective of that indifferent universe...'

In many ways, Capitalist (Hyper)Realism represents a Baudrillardian materialization. The aestheticization of the whole world requires the reality of absences as operatively transparent; today's hauntological conception is only the aestheticization of such absence. Furthermore, the aesthetics explored within this text are the aesthetics of haemorrhaging realities and the subsequent materialization of melancholia and nihilism towards an aestheticization.

If anything can become a consumer object – even absence – as Baudrillard suggests, and every object is more about the communication of addition objects, then, before we go our separate ways, allow me to channel my inner Žižekian by sharing a good Baudrillardian joke with you. Upon the gallows, amongst the spectacle of the jeering crowds, the executioner takes the capitalist aside for a moment, asking, "Why were you so foolish as to sell them the rope with which you knew they would hang you?"

"Oh, my good comrade." The capitalist smiles, knowingly. "Who do you think sold them the revolution?"

(ᴐ◔‿◔)ᴐ

'The words we call expressions of aesthetic judgement play a very complicated role, but a very definite role, in what we call a culture of a period.' Wittgenstein states in his 'Lectures on Aesthetics'. 'To describe their use or to describe what you mean by a cultured taste, you have to describe a culture.'

Sad Boy Aesthetics

This is all to say, the most revealing philosophical text of the twenty-first century could be a Socratic dialogue with Belle Delphine.[178]

Yes, Wittgenstein was right to say, 'a serious and good philosophical work could be written consisting entirely of jokes.' But as we already perceived; jokes are never about happiness. Humour inhabits the melancholia that has become our fundamental passion. You see it in the memes. In terms of aesthetics, Wittgenstein says what is; Baudrillard tells what happened.

'I should have liked to produce a good book.' Wittgenstein states in his preface to 'Philosophical Investigations.'[179] 'This has not come about, but the time is past in which I could improve it.' Likewise, consider this object only as an embodiment of my mode of disappearance from which I hope to negate my death. To find beauty somewhere in this world. A reality lived as revenge; which is to also say, the revenge aestheticized, in addition.

Selected Notes

– Sad Boy Aesthetic –

1   '…Creepypasta, bits of copy-and-paste that convey scary stories and unsettling urban Creepypasta writers take popular urban legends create entirely new subjects and fashion online stories with the intent to totally freak out the reader. They're basically short, shareable user-generated ghost stories that can focus on anything from the especially gruesome, like murder and suicide, to the creepy and otherworldly, like aliens and zombies.' Roy, Jessica. (2014). *Behind Creepypasta, the Internet Community That Allegedly Spread a Killer Meme.* Available: https://time.com/2818192/creepypasta-copypasta-slender-man/ Last accessed 6th Oct 2020. A favourite example includes the 'Lavender Town Syndrome Creepypasta' – 'The myth goes that when the first Pokémon games came out in Japan back in 1996, over 100 children who played it committed suicide. Others suffered nosebleeds or brutal headaches, or became irrationally angry when their parents asked them to take a break. Eventually, a commonality between the incidents was established—players started feeling the effects when they reached Lavender Town, home of the Pokémon graveyard, and the one dark segment in an otherwise light-hearted game.' Hill, Mark. (2016). *The Lingering Appeal of Pokémon's Greatest Ghost Story.* Available: https://web.archive.org/web/20160314190606/https://killscreen.com/articles/the-lingering-appeal-of-pokemons-greatest-ghost-story/ Last accessed 6th Oct 2020.

2   *Stardew Valley* (standard edition). 2016. Microsoft Windows, macOS, Linux, PlayStation 4, Xbox One, Nintendo Switch, PlayStation Vita, iOS, Android [Game]. ConcernedApe & Chucklefish: Seattle, Washington. Video game developed by Eric "ConcernedApe" Barone. A profoundly anti-capitalist game where the playable character escapes the hellscape of wage-slavery under the 'Joja Corporation' – 'There will come a day when you feel crushed by the burden of modern life… and your bright spirit will fade before a growing emptiness.'

3   Baudrillard, Jean. (1994). *Simulacra and Simulation*, trans. S. F. Glaser. US: The University of Michigan Press.

4   Peisner, David. (2019). *The Tragedy and Torment of Lil Peep.* Available: https://www.rollingstone.com/feature/lil-peep-tragedy-torment-804686/ Last accessed 6th Oct 2020.

5   *Everybody's Everything*, 2019, Online Streaming Service (Netflix), Benjamin Soley, US, distributed by

Gunpowder & Sky, directed by Sebastian Jones and Ramez Silyan.

6 Fisher, Mark. (2014). *Ghosts of My Life.* Hampshire: Zero Books.

7 'So where have we gone from irony? Irony is now fashionable and a widely embraced default setting for social interaction, writing and the visual arts. Irony fosters an affected nihilistic attitude […] no matter how cynical and nihilistic the times, we have always had artists who make work that invokes meaning, hope and mystery.' Ashby, Matt & Carroll, Brendan. (2014). *David Foster Wallace was right: Irony is ruining our culture.* Available: https://www.salon.com/2014/04/13/david_foster_wallace_was_right_irony_is_ruining_our_culture/ Last accessed 6th Oct 2020. According to Ashby and Carroll, Wallace optimistically calls for a 'participation over spectatorship' that may inadvertently trigger the 'possibility of something greater.' For Baudrillard, however, that participation might as well translate into the participation of a contemporary nihilism. Nothing is more participatory than the tyrannical cynicism directed towards Wallace's 'Infinite Jest'. It's a stroke of genius to position yourself as an author from which the more people criticise you with the demeanour of ironic disdain the more your analysis of the culture turns out to be true.

8 Baudrillard, Jean. (2007). *Forget Foucault*, trans. Beitchman, P, Lee Hildreth, L, & Polizzotti, M. Los Angeles: Semiotext(e). In the introduction to 'Forget Foucault', Sylvère Lotringer writes how: 'Baudrillard had become famous in America for his deadpan, seemingly nihilistic views of consumer society. Not everyone recognized him as a powerful and idiosyncratic thinker. And while he is still known today for his paradoxical positions, or extravagant formulations, not everyone realizes that these formulations derive from an impeccable philosophical core, and that their glittering effects are based on solid scholarship.'

9 Kaczynski, Theodore. (2010). *The System's Neatest Trick.* Available: https://theanarchistlibrary.org/library/ted-kaczynski-the-system-s-neatest-trick Last accessed 6th Oct 2020. As a side note, Kaczynski begins here with a quote from Jacques Ellul, 'The supreme luxury of the society of technical necessity will be to grant the bonus of useless revolt and of an acquiescent smile.' Without his Christianity, I claim Jacques

– Sad Boy Aesthetics –

Ellul is rendered a nihilist in theory. Both Kaczynski and Ellul defer nihilism through a qualitative leap in thoroughly Kierkegaardian terms. From my reading of Žižek, I have found that most people and societies defer nihilism through a similar leap towards ideology. The system's hardest trick, in thoroughly Žižekian terms, is to make the leap in the correct direction. Baudrillard, on the other hand, suggests societies' fatal leap towards the hyperreal, which is to say, the staging of transpolitical ideologies, and so on, that nonetheless seemingly negate the absences of any profound actuality.

10 'Everyone's favourite "sad bastard," Morrissey has been milking the whole mimetically nihilistic thing since 1982.' Wang, Evelyn. (2016). *A brief history of sad boy fashion*. Available: https://www.dazeddigital.com/fashion/article/32335/1/a-brief-history-of-sad-boy-fashion Last accessed 7th Oct 2020. I highly recommend Evelyn Wang's 'A brief history of sad boy fashion' which includes insights into 'ten men who kept the melancholy aesthetic alive'. 'You know the staples,' Wang writes, 'even if you think you don't: frowny faces, Japanese and Arabic as accessories, sportswear brands, Arizona iced tea, and the uncanny ability to simultaneously communicate in and be a meme. Delve too deep into Yung Lean's aesthetic and it develops a slight air of the sinister – from certain angles, it comes across as an AI simulating teenage ennui. Although his look has calmed down somewhat, his reign as this era's Prince of sadness remains unchallenged.'

11 *Silent Hill 2* (standard edition). 2001. PlayStation 2, Xbox, Microsoft Windows [Game]. Konami: Tokyo, Japan. Video game sequel developed by Team Silent in which a widower searches the town of Silent Hill for his believed to be deceased wife.

12 Hollings, Ken. (2020). *Inferno, Volume 1, The Trash Project*. London: Strange Attractor Press.

13 Yung Lean. (2013). *Yung Lean ⤳ Ginseng Strip 2002 ⤳*. Available: https://www.youtube.com/watch?v=vrQWhFysPKY Last accessed 6th Oct 2020.

14 Yung Lean. (2020). *Starz*. Available: https://www.youtube.com/playlist?list=OLAK5uy_kPH3tOCTrlrdX9bmpcWagvdjAz7Uhz4X4 Last accessed 6th Oct 2020.

15 Yung Lean. (2013). *Yung Lean - Kyoto*. Available: https://www.youtube.com/watch?v=tMgkt9jdjTU Last

accessed 6th Oct 2020.

16   Yung Lean. (2014). *Yung Lean - Yoshi City*. Available: https://www.youtube.com/watch?v=iX1a3JngmpI Last accessed 6th Oct 2020.

17   Yung Lean. (2020). *Yung Lean - Violence + Pikachu (Official Video)*. Available: https://www.youtube.com/watch?v=VamfnrmmAow Last accessed 6th Oct 2020.

18   Kerwin Frost. (2020). *KERWIN FROST TALKS TO YUNG LEAN (EPISODE 15)*. Available: https://www.youtube.com/watch?v=_SdtBslQZUQ Last accessed 6th Oct 2020.

19   ＴＲＡＳＨ新ドラゴン. (2019). *Benz Truck*. Available: https://www.youtube.com/watch?v=08Ydny8ZAzE Last accessed 6th Oct 2020.

20   ＴＲＡＳＨ新ドラゴン. (2019). *tenshi, akuma & shi*. Available: https://www.youtube.com/watch?v=cKpFli-flGQ Last accessed 6th Oct 2020.

21   ＴＲＡＳＨ新ドラゴン. (2019). *Lil peep - Star shopping (osias & kiraw remix)*. Available: https://www.youtube.com/watch?v=FBZckI6Jh3w Last accessed 6th Oct 2020.

22   'The increase in depression among young people is shocking. That should be the biggest possible indicator and condemnation of the world in which we are now living. It wasn't normal for young people to be depressed in the seventies, let's say. […] The conditions in which young people live are terrible conditions, just really terrible conditions. You've been deprived of things, and the things you've been deprived of are being sold to you as benefits. […] the nineties were a decade of the emergence of cyberspace, and of Prozac – […] these things are totally related together. How did people cope with these new levels of demands that were placed upon them? They started to take anti-depressants, which are now very common, particularly amongst young people – anti-depressants as a hazing thing. You can hear this 'downer haze'. That's why Drake is really interesting. The new Drake record, full of this electro downer haze. Everyone is on downers now to cope with the cyber blitz. Anti-depressants or other forms of self-medication in order to cope with this.' Plush Media. (2017). *Mark Fisher on why Modern Life causes Depression*. Available: https://www.youtube.com/watch?v=AhOcwhwumP4 Last accessed 7th Oct 2020.

23   AesirAesthetics. (2018). *Silent Hill 2 • Analysis (Full Commentary)*. Available: https://www.youtube.com/

watch?v=XMNwClWqexA Last accessed 7th Oct 2020.
24   Wallace, D. F. (1996). *David Lynch Keeps His Head.* Available: http://www.lynchnet.com/lh/lhpremiere.html Last accessed 7th Oct 2020.
25   Augé, Marc. (1995). *Non-Places: Introduction to an Anthropology of Supermodernity,* trans. J. Howe. London: Verso.
26   Yung Lean. (2020). *Yung Lean — Acid At 7/11 (Official Audio).* Available: https://www.youtube.com/watch?v=vYdmrLYftlI Last accessed 7th Oct 2020.
27   'The 7-Eleven brand is known and loved around the world, and our iconic products are a big part of the American culture.' 7-Eleven. (2020). *Oh Thank Heaven for 7-Eleven!.* Available: https://corp.7-eleven.com/corp/about Last accessed 7th Oct 2020.
28   drain gang. (2018). *bladee & ECCO2K - Obedient.* Available: https://www.youtube.com/watch?v=2KkMyDSrBVI Last accessed 7th Oct 2020.
29   Lil Peep. (2018). *Lil Peep - 4 GOLD CHAINS ft. Clams Casino (Official Video).* Available: https://www.youtube.com/watch?v=NEoVjmfYlJ8 Last accessed 7th Oct 2020.
30   Nenashawn Autumn. (2018). *Lil Peep - Beat It (Lyrics) [HD].* Available: https://www.youtube.com/watch?v=GnTolHNIEY4 Last accessed 7th Oct 2020.
31   Nietzsche, Friedrich. (1993). *The Birth of Tragedy from the Spirit of Music,* trans. S. Whiteside. London: Penguin Books.
32   drain gang. (2020). *bladee - Reality Surf (video).* Available: https://www.youtube.com/watch?v=xUAgawZAi5g Last accessed 7th Oct 2020.
33   Fisher, Mark. (2009). *Capitalist Realism: Is there no alternative?* Hampshire: Zero Books.
34   Сатана Dysphoric. (2017). *lil peep - star shopping (prod. kryptik).* Available: https://www.youtube.com/watch?v=qwzQPh7dW_4 Last accessed 7th Oct 2020.
35   *Chobits.* (2002). TBS, April 2.
36   *Mononoke Hime (Princess Mononoke)*, 1997, Studio Ghibli, Japan, distributed by Toho, directed by Hayao Miyazaki.
37   *Ghost in the Shell*, 1995, Production I.G, Bandai Visual, Manga Entertainment, Japan, distributed by Shochiku (Japan), Manga Entertainment (United Kingdom), directed by Mamoru Oshii.

38   *Chungking Express*, 1994, DVD, Jet Tone Production, Hong Kong, distributed by Ocean Shores Video, written and directed by Wong Kar-wai.

39   Canned products possess the heightened awareness of ephemerality. They represent the sad and melancholic desire to preserve what should naturally perish.

40   Lil Peep. (2017). *Lil Peep - Save That Shit (Official Video)*. Available: https://www.youtube.com/watch?v=WvV5TbJc9tQ Last accessed 7th Oct 2020.

41   Millard, Drew. (2016). *Is Lil Peep's Music Brilliant or Stupid as Shit?*. Available: https://www.vice.com/en/article/nznmag/is-lil-peeps-music-brilliant-or-stupid-as-shit Last accessed 7th Oct 2020.

42   *David Lynch: The Art Life*, 2017, Online Streaming Service (SkyGo), Duck Diver Films, US, directed by Jon Nguyen.

43   Noisey. (2012). *David Lynch on Twitter, Partying & Being Free*. Available: https://www.youtube.com/watch?v=UwPprWxt9oo Last accessed 7th Oct 2020.

44   Lil Peep. (2020). *Lil Peep - crybaby (Official Video)*. Available: https://www.youtube.com/watch?v=inocgEraxo0 Last accessed 7th Oct 2020.

45   'In his short life and even shorter career, the rapper born Gustav Åhr became a voice for a generation of kids who shared his powerful demons and sense of doom.' Joyce, Colin. (2019). *Lil Peep Is the Artist of the Decade*. Available: https://www.vice.com/en/article/9kejgz/lil-peep-is-the-artist-of-the-decade Last accessed 7th Oct 2020.

46   *Blade Runner*, 1982, DVD, The Ladd Company, Shaw Brothers, Blade Runner Partnership, US, distributed by Warner Bros, directed by Ridley Scott.

47   Stephanie Zaragoza. (2018). *Lil Peep - Right Here ft. Horsehead (Music Video)*. Available: https://www.youtube.com/watch?v=oXw9tYafknQ Last accessed 7th Oct 2020.

48   Lil Peep. (2020). *Lil Peep - hellboy (Official Video)*. Available: https://www.youtube.com/watch?v=s9t1ZfMZfH4 Last accessed 7th Oct 2020.

49   sadboiclique. (2018). *lil peep - haunt u [extended w/lyrics]*. Available: https://www.youtube.com/watch?v=boSjjHOvb0U Last accessed 7th Oct 2020.

50   Daniel Lopez IV. (2017). *Lil Peep - Teen Romance (Prod. Lederrick)*. Available: https://www.youtube.com/

watch?v=xUWYGfhoLj0 Last accessed 7th Oct 2020.
51   Wiggy. (2017). *lil peep x lil tracy - favorite dress (official video)*. Available: https://www.youtube.com/watch?v=Rx3szmh_Ogc Last accessed 7th Oct 2020.
52   Lil Peep. (2020). *Lil Peep - yesterday (Official Audio)*. Available: https://www.youtube.com/watch?v=qI0pJAGgbvo Last accessed 7th Oct 2020.
53   Oasis. (2013). *Oasis - Wonderwall (Official Video)*. Available: https://www.youtube.com/watch?v=bx1Bh8ZvH84 Last accessed 7th Oct 2020.
54   The Streets. (2018). *The Streets - Don't Mug Yourself (Official Video)*. Available: https://www.youtube.com/watch?v=nHs2sQOHX-0 Last accessed 7th Oct 2020.
55   Lil Peep. (2017). *Beamer Boy*. Available: https://www.youtube.com/watch?v=Sx3kDZyvnOM Last accessed 7th Oct 2020.
56   Battan, Carrie. (2018). *Lil Xan and the Year in Sad Rap*. Available: https://www.newyorker.com/magazine/2018/01/08/lil-xan-and-the-year-in-sad-rap Last accessed 7th Oct 2020.
57   Fisher, Mark. (2013). *The Secret Sadness of the 21st Century: Mark Fisher recommends James Blake's Overgrown.* Available: https://www.electronicbeats.net/mark-fisher-recommends-james-blakes-overgrown/ Last accessed 7th Oct 2020.
58   LIL UZI VERT. (2017). *Lil Uzi Vert - XO Tour Llif3 (Official Lyric Video)*. Available: https://www.youtube.com/watch?v=VcyFfcJbyeM Last accessed 7th Oct 2020.
59   Lil Peep. (2020). *Lil Peep - lil jeep (Official Video)*. Available: https://www.youtube.com/watch?v=zUPPrimH7Ow Last accessed 7th Oct 2020.
60   a-ha. (2010). *a-ha - Take On Me (Official 4K Music Video)*. Available: https://www.youtube.com/watch?v=djV11Xbc914 Last accessed 7th Oct 2020.
61   *The Ring*, 2002, DVD, MacDonald/Parkes Productions, BenderSpink, Inc, US, distributed by DreamWorks Pictures, directed by Gore Verbinski.
62   A Motorola Razr.
63   *The Joker*, 2019, Online Streaming Service (SkyGo), Warner Bros. Pictures, DC Films, Joint Effort, Bron Creative, Village Roadshow Pictures, US, distributed by Warner Bros. Pictures, directed by Todd Phillips.

64   Fisher, Mark. (2016). *The Weird and The Eerie*. London: Repeater.
65   *Blue Velvet*, 1986, Online Streaming Service (Netflix), Fred Caruso, US, distributed by De Laurentiis Entertainment Group, directed by David Lynch.
66   *Twin Peaks*. (1990–91). ABC, April 8.
67   McCaffery, Larry. (1993). *A Conversation with David Foster Wallace From "The Review of Contemporary Fiction," Summer 1993, Vol. 13.2*. Available: https://www.dalkeyarchive.com/a-conversation-with-david-foster-wallace-by-larry-mccaffery/ Last accessed 8th Oct 2020.
68   Wallace, D. F. (1998). *Laughing with Kafka*. Available: https://harpers.org/wp-content/uploads/HarpersMagazine-1998-07-0059612.pdf Last accessed 8th Oct 2020.
69   *Modern Times*, 1936, YouTube, Charlie Chaplin, US, distributed by United Artists (1936 release) Classic Entertainment (1972 release), directed by Charlie Chaplin. In 'The Self Under Siege (1993) Lecture 4: Marcuse and One-Dimensional Man', (http://rickroderick.org/304-marcuse-and-one-dimensional-man-1993/) Rick Roderick states the following in regards to Chaplin's movie: '…if you don't like these arguments that I am drawing from Marcuse, look at Charlie Chaplin movies, look at Modern Times and notice how when it was made, people could still laugh at the way Chaplin's motions matched the motions of the times, because people could remember they didn't always move like that.'
70   Lil Peep. (2018). *Lil Peep - Life Is Beautiful*. Available: https://www.youtube.com/watch?v=2ORsrbQa94M Last accessed 8th Oct 2020.
71   MYSTIC PIMP. (2016). *Lil Peep - About U*. Available: https://www.youtube.com/watch?v=IjebaddTUsI Last accessed 8th Oct 2020.
72   Lil Peep. (2019). *Lil Peep - ghost boy (Official Audio)*. Available: https://www.youtube.com/watch?v=NiWFVHbB_Eo Last accessed 8th Oct 2020.
73   *Hot Fuzz*, 2007, DVD, StudioCanal, Working Title Films, Big Talk Productions, UK, distributed by Universal Pictures, directed by Edgar Wright.
74   *The World's End*, 2013, DVD, Relativity Media, StudioCanal, Working Title Films, Big Talk Pictures, UK, distributed by Universal Pictures, directed by Edgar Wright.

75   Angelo Badalamenti. (2017). *Twin Peaks Theme (Instrumental).* Available: https://www.youtube.com/watch?v=Z30zg9a5M5k Last accessed 8th Oct 2020.

76   Kuba Stawicki. (2012). *Akira Yamaoka Silent Hill 2 Original Soundtracks.* Available: https://www.youtube.com/watch?v=QFvt2cNSOaM Last accessed 8th Oct 2020.

77   'Ghosting — when someone cuts off all communication without explanation — extends to all things, it seems. Most of us think about it in the context of digital departure: a friend not responding to a text, or worse, a lover, but it happens across all social circumstances and it's tied to the way we view the world. […] A ghost is a specter, something we think is there but really isn't. We've all probably acted like this if we're honest. We've all probably been ghosted, too, though sometimes we probably didn't notice. These are supernatural times.' Popescu, Adam. (2019). *Why People Ghost — and How to Get Over It.* Available: https://www.nytimes.com/2019/01/22/smarter-living/why-people-ghost-and-how-to-get-over-it.html Last accessed 8th Oct 2020.

78   Lil Peep. (2020). *Lil Peep - big city blues (feat. cold hart) (Official Audio).* Available: https://www.youtube.com/watch?v=6ViiarPAoYY Last accessed 8th Oct 2020.

79   Lil Peep. (2020). *Lil Peep - nineteen (Official Audio).* Available: https://www.youtube.com/watch?v=YkvekRdhIgg Last accessed 8th Oct 2020.

80   The following essay was originally published at the 'International Academic Journal Baudrillard Now'. (Mazey, Alexzander. (2021). Baudrillard's Pendulum. International Academic Journal Baudrillard Now. Volume 2, Issue 1.

'Baudrillard's Pendulum'

'Conspiracies do exist.'

Umberto Eco

A Coca-Cola billboard appears, only very briefly, above the American town of Hope, Washington, in the 1982 film, '*First Blood*'. (1982, Online Streaming Service (SkyGo), Anabasis Investments, N.V., US, distributed by Orion Pictures, directed by Ted Kotcheff. (Buzz Feitshans is credited as the producer for this film).) Interestingly enough, this billboard (the domestic soft power) is elevated above Will Teasle, the sheriff of the town (the domestic hard power, so to speak) who pursues (haunts) John Rambo throughout the film, significant, perhaps, as elevating Coca-Cola above all things in American life.

Isn't it interesting how the final scenes of *'First Blood'* show Stallone putting an end to the billboards and advertisements that litter the landscape of this quaint, thoroughly American, township? Isn't this another example of domestic 'soft power' meeting the 'hard power' of a rifle; a co-opted 'hard power', so to speak? It is striking, the way John Rambo, through sheer will and violence (a violence manifesting as an inability to communicate the crimes of imperialism), removes these corrupted artifices of capitalist America or, at the very least, those that litter this small-town landscape.

John Rambo's sense of righteousness in *'First Blood'* – as with all moral righteousness – leads to a sentence of hard labour at the hands of *Criminal* Justice. This lays the groundwork for *'Rambo: First Blood Part II'* (1985, Online Streaming Service (SkyGo), Anabasis Investments, N.V., US, distributed by TriStar Pictures (US), Thorn EMI Screen Entertainment (UK) directed by George P. Cosmatos. (Buzz Feitshans is credited as the producer for this film.)) whereby we observe Colonel Sam Trautman meeting John at a prison-labour camp, asking for help.

Slavoj Žižek provides a good overview of this second film, where we see Rambo travelling to Vietnam to save a group of veterans from a Soviet backed outfit of militia. In an interview with Josefina Ayerza, published in 'Lusitania' in the Fall of 1994', Žižek says about the film:

'In the United States, I was struck by the series of films like Rambo […] which are based on the American obsession that there are still some prisoners, some Americans alive down there in Vietnam. The hero, Rambo, saves them, brings them back. I think the fantasy behind it is that the most precious part of America was stolen and the hero brings it back to where it belongs. Because this "treasure" was missing under Jimmy Carter, America was weak. If the hero brings it back, America will be strong again.' (https://www.lacan.com/perfume/Zizekinter.htm)

In other words, after dismantling the quiet town of Hope, Washington – littered with its corporate artifice – Rambo seeks to return something to America that has been lost, years ago, in the jungles of Vietnam. What has been lost here, in these jungles, other than some 'nostalgic referential', a sense of humanity, something to point the way forward, a love for something beyond the commodities of a *lost* America.

Once again, the commodity is located within the sign-values of Coca-Cola, a drink that features heavily in the mise en scène of *'Rambo: First Blood Part II'*, particularly within the military operations base, where we observe generals glugging away at Coca-Cola, (cans of Coke, chilled in a vending machine, no less), alongside the blinking lights of unrecognisable technologies; computers and equipment which Rambo will come to destroy in another scene of spectacular vengeance.

Even so, what does Rambo find in his return to the jungles of Vietnam? Love, of course. Not the love of a commodity, full of 'metaphysical nasties', but rather the love of a living, breathing, human being. A living referential for what America has lost in its desire for imperialistic conquest. Isn't it interesting how Rambo finds his unbeknownst love, his assigned contact, Co Bao, as he passes through a littered landscape of lost, Buddhist (I assume) relics? Here, I am reminded of Mark Fisher's analysis of those stone statues on Easter Island.

In *'The Weird and the Eerie'*, (Fisher, Mark. (2016). *The Weird and The Eerie*. London: Repeater) Fisher writes:

> 'The problem here is not why the people who created these structures disappeared – there is no mystery here – but the nature of what disappeared. What kinds of being created these structures? How were they similar to us, and how were they different? What kind of symbolic order did these beings belong to, and what role did the monuments they constructed play in it? For the symbolic structures which made sense of the monuments have rotted away, and in a sense what we witness here is the unintelligibility and inscrutability of the Real itself. Confronted with Easter Island or Stonehenge, it is hard not to speculate about what the relics of our culture will look like when the semiotic systems in which they are currently embedded have fallen away.'

This is – perhaps – Fisher's greatest insight, where he came to locate the source of his own hauntological circumstance as an experience originating from dwindling points of reference. The residue of a world 'rotted away'. In some sense, we can consider the Britain of Fisher's youth – full of subcultural vibrancy and rave culture – as his own Easter Island, put to death by the enemy of neoliberal values inherent in the prevailing capitalist (hyper)realism of the twenty-first century.

Nothing is more painful than the lost referential, *monuments out of time*, divorced from the semiotic systems that once governed them. It is an intriguing question to ask what would be lost from our own structures if not the order of the hyperreal that governs them; the irreality of sign-value and the like? Would Wall Street not look sepulchral without the virtual territorialization of 'transeconomic' metastasis? All around us, cities like ready-built tombs.

Even so, it is never a case of what has been lost, it is always more important to observe what has been left behind; to view the lost in relation to what's left behind is nostalgia incarnate. Nevertheless, to consider what has been left behind is perhaps more painful than to consider what has been taken away. Isn't this the melancholy that drives both Mark Fisher *and* John Rambo? After all, he is not angry at what has been taken away from him – he is angry at *what's left*; a vapidity of existence, a shallow and passive nihilism, which is to say, a position we could characterise as Baudrillard's 'terminal melancholy'. (Fisher, Mark. (1999). *Flatline constructs: Gothic materialism and cybernetic theory-fiction.* PhD thesis, University of Warwick.)

This is why Rambo seeks comfort in the silence and depth of a spiritual Buddhism, perhaps? It is fascinating how Buddhism – and its icons – feature in every Rambo film, aside from *'First Blood'*, the one film grounded in the landscape of America. After all, with its penchant for silence, how could Buddhism exist in a utopia built on the foundations of an endless and ecstatic communication, other than by way of simulation and image?

One of the more prescient expositions of the dynamic interplay between Coca-Cola and Buddhism appears in *'Rambo III'* (1988, Online Streaming Service (SkyGo), Carolco Pictures, US, distributed by TriStar Pictures, directed by Peter MacDonald. (Buzz Feitshans is credited as the producer for this film.)) In the opening scene, as John prepares for a prize-fight, shots of Buddhist monks are interjected alongside scenes of Colonel Sam Trautman walking from the American Embassy of Thailand. As the Colonel strides through the market bizarre, we see the distinct Coca-Cola logo, the 'soft power' of American capitalist values – as it always appears in

– Sad Boy Aesthetics –

the 'developing' world – integrated neatly into the sign-value system of the local marketplace.

Likewise, in the early cinematic adaptation of *'Total Recall'*, (1990, Online Streaming Service (SkyGo), Carolco Pictures, US, distributed by TriStar Pictures, directed by Paul Verhoeven. (Buzz Feitshans is credited as the producer for this film.)) Coca-Cola appears as a billboard advertisement within the 'future' world of the Philip K. Dick novel, which can today be read as a theory-fiction into the nature of the hyperreal trajectory. Later on, in the 1995 adaption of *'Judge Dredd'*, (1995, Online Streaming Service (SkyGo), Hollywood Pictures, Cinergi Pictures, Edward R. Pressman Film Corporation, US, distributed by Buena Vista Pictures (North America/South America) Cinergi Productions (International), directed by Danny Cannon. (Buzz Feitshans had joined Cinergi Productions in 1992.)) Coca-Cola would appear, once again, this time in the 'cursed lands', where a Coke bottle appears – both strikingly and briefly – to be stood on in the desert wastelands of a futuristic America.

In terms of Baudrillardian analysis, *'First Blood'* tells the story of the commodities' dominion, 'the domestic battle' over the American landscape, where the commodity has finally 'overcome' humanism, negating the alternative philosophies of depth and silence inherent in the spiritual posturing of Buddhism, for example. Both *'Rambo: First Blood Part II'* and *'Rambo III'* tell the story of a 'globalisation', a confrontation between the individual – with all its spiritual grotesquery – against the ecstatic delights of the commodity's materialization. This is Coca-Cola as a harbinger of the hyperreal, finding fruition in *'Judge Dredd'*, through which we glimpse our 'cursed' future; our desert of the real.

Of course, if you think I am over-reaching, just remember how the *'Rambo Trilogy of the Eighties'*, and *'Judge Dredd'*, all feature Sylvester Stallone as title characters. (Aside from the film – *'First Bloo*d' – where the commodity has already prevailed over the human subject of small-town America; the commodity has already drawn 'first blood', so to speak.) The smoking gun of this theory can be found in Buzz Feitshans, the executive producer of all five films discussed, here.

In conclusion, we have the appearances of the exact same commodity, a similar casting, the exact same executive producer; how much of this is purely coincidental? These five films, all produced by Feitshans, actually tell a meta-narrative of Coca-Cola dominating small town American life in *'First Blood'*, before representing the beverage as a product of colonial hard power in *'Rambo: First Blood Part II'*, then as a global consumer object of soft power in *'Rambo III'*, before featuring in the dystopian landscape of Philip K. Dick's *'Total Recall'*, and finding a fruition of its trajectory as a product of the hyperreal order in the desert of the 'cursed earth' in *'Judge Dredd'*. It seems we are given, in these films, a meta-narrative regarding the perverse omnipresence of the commodity; the mythological trajectory of Coca-Cola itself.

I would also like to mention John McTiernan's masterpiece, *'Die Hard'* (1988, Online Streaming Service (SkyGo), Gordon Company, Silver Pictures, US, distributed by 20th Century Fox, directed by John McTiernan. (Cinergi Pictures would go on to produce *'Die Hard with a Vengeance'* in 1995.)) What is John McClane (Bruce Willis) – the hero and protagonists – other than a Linkolan 'Guardian of Life', operating chiefly as another cinematic recurrence of a 'masculine referential', a character (a police cop, nonetheless) ostracised from the hyperreal 'corporate' world; a man who understands the sacrifices that need to be made in an attempt to preserve life? Ironically, during the climax – in order to the save his estranged wife (Bonnie Bedelia), the damsel, from the clutches of a 'referential evil', Hans Gruber (Alan Rickman) – John sacrifices an expensive, personalised Rolex watch. Is this scene not loaded with a powerful meta-significance? The sign-value significance given over to that commodity, particularly in the scene between Hans Gruber and Harry Ellis, is truly fascinating.

It is amusing how Harry Ellis – a stereotypical, morally relativistic, corporate cocaine addict – askes the terrorists for a Coca-Cola. It is interesting how Coca-Cola becomes a signifier of Ellis' hallucinatory notions of coked-up power. Compare, for example, in that final scene between Ellis and Gruber, the interplay between the impotence of Ellis' chosen commodity (a referential soft power) compared to the force of Gruber's handgun (a referential hard power). Isn't it interesting how Gruber's hard power is only overcome by the 'nostalgic referential' – the American hard power – in other words, a previously ostracised, 'sheriff's justice' – finding representation in John McClane? In overcoming Gruber's terroristic plot, McClane must concede the 'soft power' of the Rolex watch. Gruber's corrupted desire for commodities – stealing negotiable bearer bonds to purchase additional 'John Philips' suits in London, I imagine – has to be mediated by a thoroughly 'Americanised' sense of justice. In this way, *'Die Hard'* is a deeply propagandistic film; but a great action flick, nonetheless. It is Alan Rickman's greatest performance, perhaps? second only to his portrayal of the Sheriff of Nottingham in *'Robin Hood: Prince of Thieves'* (1991, Online Streaming Service (Netflix), Morgan Creek Productions, US, distributed by Warner Bros., directed by Kevin Reynolds.) A film where the thoroughly corrupted morality of (Christian) justice, lost in the capture of Jerusalem by the army of Saladin, must be returned to England in the form of Robin of Locksley (Kevin Costner).

Even so, the portrayal of Coca-Cola as a means of 'hallucinatory power' – the 'sign-value' of this particular commodity, (particularly as a means of soft power) – is prevalent throughout the mise en scène of many 80s' action films; perhaps most strikingly in the 80s' 'Rambo' trilogy, featuring Sylvester Stallone as US Army veteran, John Rambo. It should be noted how, much like Arnold Schwarzenegger, Sylvester Stallone has developed, over the years, into a 'transcendental referential'; in other words, a referential that transcends the limits of the cinematic fiction. He had – in terms of the hyperreal – come to represent the 'nostalgic referential' of hypermasculinity in particular, even outside the remit of the cinema screen. If you want additional examples of Stallone's hyperreal credentials, one only has to visit the Smithsonian Museum of America, where you will find a multitude of props from *'Rocky'* (1976, Online Streaming Service (Netflix), Chartoff-Winkler Productions, US, distributed by United Artists, directed by John G. Avildsen.) selected by the Library of Congress as culturally significant, worthy of preservation and so on. Alternatively, you could consider Rocky Balboa's inclusion into the 'International Boxing Hall of Fame'. Not bad achievements for someone who does not really exist, but rather retains a presence, a residue, in thoroughly simulated forms; in other words, exists as a point of reference, the 'idealised American man', in this case.

In terms of Baudrillardian analysis, the fictionalised account of the 'American Dream', portrayed in *'Rocky'*, and its five sequels, actually masks the reality of its total absence in American life. Here, I will recall to your mind the words of America's greatest intellectual, George Carlin: 'The owners of this country know the truth; it's called the American Dream because you have to be asleep to believe it.'

What we lack in a simulated reality, we make up for in fiction. Isn't this the hidden motivation behind the 80s' 'Rambo' trilogy, for example? A film where the downtrodden, Vietnam veteran is able to exercise his fantasies through an aestheticized vengeance, initially, upon small town America, *'First Blood'* (1982), and later, an American military base of operations, *'Rambo: First Blood Part II'* (1985). It is fascinating how this all-American hero later fights in the Soviet–Afghan War, fighting alongside the Mujahideen, no less, in *'Rambo III'* (1988). Nothing is more painfully ironic, these days, than to observe the final commemoration of that film, whereby we see *'Rambo III'* dedicated 'to the gallant people of Afghanistan.' Interestingly enough, a rumour circulates, (a conspiracy theory of sorts) claiming the film's commemoration once read 'to the brave Mujahideen fighters', with alterations taking place in response to the September 11 attacks. Will we ever really know the truth in regards to this rumour's persistence? More importantly – it begs the question – do we believe our mythology is beyond such revisionism?

81   cold hart. (2020). *Cold Hart & Lil Peep - "Me and You"*. Available: https://www.youtube.com/watch?v=uFloXhFcsNE Last accessed 8th Oct 2020

82   Kellner, Douglas. (2005, revised in 2019). *Jean Baudrillard*. Available: https://plato.stanford.edu/entries/baudrillard/ Last accessed 8th Oct 2020.

83   Lil Peep. (2018). *Lil Peep & XXXTENTACION - Falling Down*. Available: https://www.youtube.com/watch?v=-jRKsiAOAA8 Last accessed 8th Oct 2020.

84   Lyrical Lemonade. (2018). *Juice WRLD - Lucid Dreams (Dir. by @_ColeBennett_)*. Available: https://www.youtube.com/watch?v=mzB1VGEGcSU Last accessed 8th Oct 2020.

85   Sting. (2018). *Shape Of My Heart*. Available: https://www.youtube.com/watch?v=dOjFcx3GJHg Last accessed 8th Oct 2020.

86   Lewis, P. H. (1994). *Attention Shoppers: Internet Is Open*. Available: https://www.nytimes.com/1994/08/12/business/attention-shoppers-internet-is-open.html Last accessed 8th

Oct 2020.
87   Lil Peep. (2019). *Lil Peep -- 16 Lines (Official Video).* Available: https://www.youtube.com/watch?v=DxNt7xV5aII Last accessed 8th Oct 2020.
88   Lil Peep. (2017). *Lil Peep - Awful Things ft. Lil Tracy (Official Video).* Available: https://www.youtube.com/watch?v=zOujzvtwZ6M Last accessed 8th Oct 2020.
89   Lil Peep. (2017). *witchblades - lil peep x lil tracy.* Available: https://www.youtube.com/watch?v=E7sP6t1QyrI Last accessed 8th Oct 2020.
90   Lil Peep. (2017). *Lil Peep - The Brightside.* Available: https://www.youtube.com/watch?v=xAMgQQMZ9Lk Last accessed 8th Oct 2020.
91   Žižek, Slavoj. (2014). *Trouble in Paradise.* London: Allen Lane.
92   .sad 悲しい. (2016). *LiL PEEP - i crash, u crash (ft. Lil Tracy) [prod. Jayyeah].* Available: https://www.youtube.com/watch?v=XsZGjzpknlQ Last accessed 8th Oct 2020.
93   *Sen to Chihiro no Kamikakushi (Spirited Away)*, 2001, Studio Ghibli, Japan, distributed by Toho, directed by Hayao Miyazaki.
94   Lil Peep. (2020). *Lil Peep - driveway (Official Audio).* Available: https://www.youtube.com/watch?v=teMZk4bCgSw Last accessed 9th Oct 2020.
95   *Manhunt: Unabomber.* (2017). Discovery Channel, August 1.
96   デーモンAstari. (2015). *LiL PEEP - The Way I See Things.* Available: https://www.youtube.com/watch?v=1OW9K84EbU4 Last accessed 9th Oct 2020.
97   'A film that's a classic film that shows it is Dr Strangelove – ah, wonderful performance with Peter Sellers, great movie, if you haven't seen it, please see it; directed by Stanley Kubrick – in which one of the most famous examples of rationality under this heading occurs, and that's the arms race. Both sides keep building and building and building and building and building, and every move by one side calls forth a rational move by the other. The only problem is that if it continued the outcome would not have been rational, far from it… far from it. […] Now let me give you a classic one that even analytical philosophers know about, it's in Game Theory. That's something analytical philosophers love: game theory, it's beautiful for them. It's called the paradox of the

dams. [Roderick explains the paradox of the dams]. Now I have gone through this at some length because this is going to be the heart of a criticism of modern technological society that Marcuse will raise. This is at the heart of his criticism. It is not his criticism that our society should just throw away instrumental reason; should just give up on thinking scientifically, that's not it at all. It's that if we don't find a more balanced approach to ourselves, our world, other people, than instrumental rationality – we are lost.' Roderick, Rick. (2010). *304 Marcuse and One-Dimensional Man (1993)*. Available: http://rickroderick.org/304-marcuse-and-one-dimensional-man-1993/ Last accessed 9th Oct 2020.

98   *Twelve Monkeys*, 1995, Online Streaming Service (Netflix), Atlas Entertainment, Classico, US, distributed by Universal Pictures, directed by Terry Gilliam.

99   Lil Peep. (2017). *lil peep - benz truck (prod. smokeasac)*. Available: https://www.youtube.com/watch?v=3rkJ3L5Ce80 Last accessed 9th Oct 2020.

100   Yung Lean. (2020). *Yung Lean x Bladee - Opium Dreams*. Available: https://www.youtube.com/watch?v=EdzmSiYooEg Last accessed 9th Oct 2020.

101   Sartre, Jean-Paul. (2000). *Nausea,* trans. Baldick, R. England: Penguin Books.

102   Orapello, Christopher & Maguire, Tara-Love. (2018). *Besom, Stang & Sword*. Canada: Weiser Books.

103   The Radical Revolution. (2019). *Slavoj Zizek — Atheist Christianity.* Available: https://www.youtube.com/watch?v=TEuY46p5yH4 Last accessed 9th Oct 2020.

104   Quiet Cam. (2016). *LIL PEEP - PRAYING TO THE SKY (LIVE)*. Available: https://www.youtube.com/watch?v=2YErDmoAsMU Last accessed 9th Oct 2020.

105   *On the Waterfront*, 1954, Online Streaming Service (SkyGo), Horizon Pictures, US, distributed by Columbia Pictures Corporation, directed by Elia Kazan.

106   *It's a Wonderful Life*, 1946, DVD, Liberty Films, US, distributed by RKO Radio Pictures, directed by Frank Capra.

107   Nenashawn Autumn. (2018). *Lil Peep - Give U The Moon (Lyrics) [HD]*. Available: https://www.youtube.com/watch?v=b6TE_x7HIhI Last accessed 9th Oct 2020.

108   Lil Peep. (2020). *Lil Peep - ghost girl (Official Audio)*. Available:https://www.youtube.com/watch?v=pcFK4HzAlsU Last accessed 9th Oct 2020.

109   A distinction should be made between the 'the other nihilism', which could be read as the passive nihilism of the system verses the active nihilism of Baudrillardian critique, and so on. These are Nietzschean ideals, of course. A dichotomy that is disintegrated, perhaps, within the aesthetic itself. This is to say, sad boy aesthetics interrogates the value of an active nihilism in a world of passive nihilism. In terms of passive and active nihilism: is it even possible to distinguish between the two anymore?

110   GordonYYZ. (2009). *Trooper – We're Here For A Good Time (Not A Long Time).* Available: https://www.youtube.com/watch?v=8gCjJC_INNE Last accessed 9th Oct 2020.

111   Lil Peep. (2017). *Lil Peep - U Said [Audio].* Available: https://www.youtube.com/watch?v=8pGbGjSD9kA Last accessed 9th Oct 2020.

112   Lil Peep. (2018). *Lil Peep - Runaway (Official Video).* Available: https://www.youtube.com/watch?v=zMCVp6INpnw Last accessed 9th Oct 2020.

113   Baudrillard, Jean. (1993). *The Transparency of Evil,* trans. Benedict, J. London: Verso.

114   Lil Peep. (2016). *lil peep - gym class.* Available: https://www.youtube.com/watch?v=heJNHYCSsIc Last accessed 9th Oct 2020.

115   Words taken from 'The Crunch' by Charles Bukowski. A YouTube edit of this poem features scenes taken from Wong Kar-wai's 'Chungking Express'. illneas. (2018). *People Aren't Good (The Crunch by Charles Bukowski).* Available: https://www.youtube.com/watch?v=pgG88p7F98c Last accessed 9th Oct 2020.

116   Nenashawn Autumn. (2018). *Lil Peep - Beat It (Lyrics) [HD].* Available: https://www.youtube.com/watch?v=GnTolHNIEY4 Last accessed 9th Oct 2020.

117   Hagberg, Garry. (2007, revised 2014). *Wittgenstein's Aesthetics.* Available: https://plato.stanford.edu/entries/wittgenstein-aesthetics/ Last accessed 9th Oct 2020.

118   'If we imagine the dream realized, we'd not thereby have solved what we feel to be aesthetic puzzlements, although we may be able to predict that a certain line of poetry will, on a certain person, act in such and such a way. What we really want, to solve aesthetic puzzlements, is certain comparisons- grouping together of certain cases.' Wittgenstein, Ludwig. (1966). *Lectures and Conversations on Aesthetics, Psychology, and*

Religious Belief, ed. Cyril Barrett. Oxford: Basil Blackwell.

119 yokeo. (2015). *lil peep - veins (prod. greaf).* Available: https://www.youtube.com/watch?v=0VaeyqMK0GU Last accessed 9th Oct 2020.

120 Joji. (2020 updated). *BALLADS 1.* Available: https://www.youtube.com/playlist?list=PLzjD-HnzMfXJPjD8f0r3F2Iu1X4h7eTOP Last accessed 9th Oct 2020.

121 88rising. (2018). *Joji - YEAH RIGHT.* Available: https://www.youtube.com/watch?v=tG7wLK4aAOE Last accessed 9th Oct 2020.

122 88rising. (2018). *Joji - SLOW DANCING IN THE DARK.* Available: https://www.youtube.com/watch?v=K3Qzzggn--s Last accessed 9th Oct 2020.

123 88rising. (2018). *Joji - WANTED U (Official Audio).* Available: https://www.youtube.com/watch?v=z9gVoelEjws Last accessed 9th Oct 2020.

124 88rising. (2018). *Joji - TEST DRIVE.* Available: https://www.youtube.com/watch?v=PEBS2jbZce4 Last accessed 9th Oct 2020.

125 88rising. (2018). *Joji ft. Clams Casino - CAN'T GET OVER YOU.* Available: https://www.youtube.com/watch?v=zbxAB7rTpDc Last accessed 9th Oct 2020.

126 88rising. (2018). *Joji - ATTENTION (Official Audio).* Available: https://www.youtube.com/watch?v=ulMHhPHYCi0 Last accessed 9th Oct 2020.

127 Yung Lean's 'Pikachu' (Available: https://www.youtube.com/watch?v=2IkulUI9llc Last accessed 9th Oct 2020) is another good example of recalling this cultural period, as is a track like 'Hennessy & Sailor Moon' featuring Bladee. (Available: https://www.youtube.com/watch?v=5qfP7a9UcuY Last accessed 9th Oct 2020.) In terms of a good visual example, for comparison, refer to the official video for Bladee's 'Reality Surf'. (Available: https://www.youtube.com/watch?v=xUAgawZAi5g Last accessed 9th Oct 2020.)

128 88rising. (2018). *Joji ft. Trippie Redd - R.I.P. (Official Audio).* Available: https://www.youtube.com/watch?v=AwHIYWKvoEE Last accessed 9th Oct 2020.

129 88rising. (2018). *Joji - NO FUN (Official Audio).* Available: https://www.youtube.com/watch?v=8Vlej7QUGGE Last accessed 9th Oct 2020.

130   Nihilism is an ontology that can infer a range of emotional responses. Nothing about nihilism denies an emotional response to existence. It merely suggests those emotions are all equally worthless. Pessimism and existential dread can become the symptomatic occurrence at the point of a nihilistic revelation. We should move past the idea that pessimism/dread and the related opposites, in addition, are mutually exclusive to an ontology based on nihilism. Nonetheless, nihilism continues to be poorly represented in popular culture. Nihilists seem to slide gradually towards nihilism, rather than waking up one morning as self-described nihilists, which explains why so much of the nihilistic ontology is clouded by a remit of misconception. There's also the dichotomy of active/passive nihilism that adds an additional layer of confusion. As a consequence, people often assume a position of 'Popular Nihilism', (a thoroughly hyperreal conception, so to speak), that has largely diverted from what we might consider the Nietzschean dialectic.

131   デーモンAstari. (2016). *LiL PEEP - Five Degrees // prod. Haardtek.* Available: https://www.youtube.com/watch?v=Y8dihA5xuKg Last accessed 9th Oct 2020.

132   drain gang. (2016). *bladee - Sugar.* Available: https://www.youtube.com/watch?v=r8BYL-vHZxo Last accessed 9th Oct 2020.

133   Yung Lean. (2016). *Yung Lean - Hennessy & Sailor Moon (feat. bladee).* Available: https://www.youtube.com/watch?v=5qfP7a9UcuY Last accessed 9th Oct 2020.

134   Ligotti, Thomas. (2018). *The Conspiracy Against the Human Race.* New York: Penguin Books.

135   Lil Peep. (2018). *Lil Peep - 4 GOLD CHAINS ft. Clams Casino (Official Video).* Available: https://www.youtube.com/watch?v=NEoVjmfYlJ8 Last accessed 9th Oct 2020.

136   Lil Peep. (2016). *LIL PEEP & LIL TRACY - COBAIN OFFICIAL VIDEO.* Available: https://www.youtube.com/watch?v=K87vhWtIz9g Last accessed 9th Oct 2020.

137   A lot can be said about icons and their narcissism. On page sixty-five of 'Flatline Constructs', Mark Fisher suggests that 'Baudrillard's Narcissism designates a condition in which selves collapse into their images; Baudrillard invokes a "digital narcissus, [who] is going to slide along the trajectory of a death drive and sink in his own image."' With additional reference to 'Flatline Constructs', Mark Fisher's thinking can

be read as a failed attempt 'to move beyond Baudrillard's position of terminal melancholy.'

138 The Smiths. (2018). *The Smiths - I Know Its Over*. Available: https://www.youtube.com/watch?v=M6o1SEj02t0 Last accessed 9th Oct 2020.

139 The Smiths. (2015). *Last Night I Dreamt That Somebody Loved Me (2011 Remaster)*. Available: https://www.youtube.com/watch?v=4WCnl1VTEeg Last accessed 9th Oct 2020.

140 Nirvana. (2009). *Nirvana - In Bloom (Official Video)*. Available: https://www.youtube.com/watch?v=PbgKEjNBHqM Last accessed 9th Oct 2020.

141 One beauty of Nirvana could be located in how no one was ever really sure what Cobain was communicating within his lyrics; I think there was a joke being played on people who thought they did understand.

142 Nirvana. (2020). *MTV Unplugged In New York*. Available: https://www.youtube.com/playlist?list=OLAK5uy_khF-bYQKOZrX9U1WH0-7z1xzssUd4q4_I Last accessed 9th Oct 2020.

143 Jean Baudrillard, Florian Rötzer. (2020). "Things Surpass Themselves". *International Academic Journal, Baudrillard Now*. Volume 1, Issue 2 (1), p5 - 14.

144 Someone replaced the book jacket image of Nick Land's 'Fanged Noumena' with the cover art from Bladee's album '333', as if drawing attention to the accelerative nature of these two prescient artefacts. The meme in question seemed to highlight the convergence between the philosophy of acceleration and the drain gang aesthetic which desperately sought to drive a culture elsewhere.

In 'Postcapitalist Desire' (Fisher, Mark. (2021). *Postcapitalist Desire*. London: Repeater), Mark Fisher would define Land's idea of 'capitalistic accelerationism' as 'the most intense force ever to exist on earth – that the whole of terrestrial history had led to the emergence of this effectively planetary artificial intelligence system which therefore can be seen as retrospectively guiding all history towards its own emergence – a bit like Skynet in the *Terminator* films.' The question Matt Colquhoun reiterated in his introduction to Fisher's 'Postcapitalist Desire' lectures would be whether or not society really wanted 'to push beyond capitalism?' Through the very formulation of this question, Fisher would perhaps begin to envision 'a new praxis for a left-accelerationism.'

Fisher's Accelerationism would never be entirely uncoupled from Land's 'capitalistic accelerationism', however, with the atmosphere of the moralising Left often falling for the '(perhaps fatal)' associations Colquhoun would also lean towards within his own introduction. Even so, the introduction to 'Postcapitalist Desire' would offer no intellectually satisfying or direct severance between Fisher and the Landian ideas of acceleration, defined here in cultural terms, especially.

Perhaps very few thinkers have the impertinence to say what Fisher was really thinking; if accelerationism was not repurposed by a conscious Left to bring about an alternative system, it would be co-opted – not by the spectre of a kooky fringe Right – but by the very locatable threat Slavoj Žižek would identify as 'barbarism with a human face.'

Similar to Land's 'intense poeticization of the power of capital', Bladee's 'Mallwhore Freestyle' from the 'Icedancer' album (drain gang. (2018). *bladee (sponsored by RipSquaD) ICEDANCER **MIXTAPE***. Available: https://www.youtube.com/watch?v=GxgNFCWL_zg Last accessed 18th Feb 2021.) represents a similar poetic intensity. The 'libidinal infrastructure' of capital is evident from the very juxtaposition of the titular words 'Mall' and 'Whore' with the 'Freestyle' addition simulating the essence of 'off the dome' rap. In strictly Baudrillardian terms, however, 'Mallwhore Freeestyle' is a track dealing with 'The Consumer Society' (Baudrillard, Jean. (1998). *The Consumer Society*. London: SAGE Publications) and 'The System of Objects' (Baudrillard, Jean. (1996). *The System of Objects*, trans. James Benedict. London: Verso) – Prada and Tom Ford – sign-values and sham objects.

In the opening essay which accompanied the translation of 'The Consumer Society', George Ritzer would write how Baudrillard 'clearly felt that we had moved into an era dominated by the exchange of sign-values.' Ritzer continues, 'When looked at from a structural perspective, what we consume is signs (messages, images) rather than commodities. This means that consumers need to be able to 'read' the system of consumption in order to know what to consume. Furthermore, because we all know the 'code', we know the meaning of the consumption of one commodity rather than another. Commodities are no longer defined by their use, but rather by what they signify. And what they signify is defined not by what they do, but by their relationship to the entire system of commodities and signs.' This would offer a good overview of what Baudrillard had already begun to explore in earlier texts with the later Baudrillard focusing – with increasingly nihilistic perspective – on how individuals, in the words of Ritzer, 'are coerced into using that system.' Ritzer finally concludes how '[t]he ideology associated with the system leads people to believe, falsely in Baudrillard's view, that they are affluent, fulfilled, happy and liberated.'

Within Bladee's 'Mallwhore Freeestyle' we perceive a speaker who has been thoroughly coerced into the system of sign-values, an unconvincing (post-ironic) subject of 'enjoyment or pleasure'. The subject of the lyrics operates as an 'institutionalized' agent; a 'mallwhore' whose manufactured desire for difference seeks the potential realisation through the system of signs offered by luxury branding. The 'Prada backpack', 'Tom Ford', 'black Porsche', 'Fendi', 'Louis [Vuitton]' and 'Dior' 'stores' all feature as signs within a 'game' of 'this Drain life…' realised, in Baudrillardian terms as 'a synthesis of consumer activities, not the least of which are shopping, flirting with objects, playful wandering and all the permutational possibilities of these.'

The permutation of 'Mallwhore Freeestyle' embodies a flirtation, the 'playful wandering' of smelling 'like weed in the Prada store', 'gettin' free shit in Fendi stores' and 'Prada backpackin'' in the Louis store'. The ecstatic succession of the ballad, dripping with a limerent romanticism, finds continuation in the 'Boing!' of 'I hit Dior'.

As the speaker becomes increasingly submerged by the communication of these sign-values, they come to lose something of an authentic self-expression, whilst divulging an ironic state of solipsistic alienation:

> 'she say I should talk more / I can't even talk more, you should check the scoreboard'. The 'wandering' acts of consumption, which is in itself a type of empty and directionless searching, is eventually experienced as this virtual reality 'game' first finding representation within the imagery of a 'scoreboard' before later confirmed entirely: 'This Drain life, I'm about it / I'm the founder, yeah, I found it / Play the game, yeah, I foul it.'

It seems as if the speaker is beginning to lose touch with

the environment of the pronoun, the real name of this 'girl' becoming lost behind the litany of brand names. There is an obvious prioritising of the potentially signified narcissism of the body, achieved through the sign-values of luxury goods, over the very real and human relationship, in fact, everyone soon becomes implicated here since, 'My girl said she need some shit too'.

The lyrical conceptualisation of 'shit' is humorous since it recalls in my mind Jean-François Lyotard's 'shit of capital'. As Lyotard predicted in his 'evil book', even contemporary intellectuals, and I quote, 'dare not say that the only important thing there is to say, that one can enjoy swallowing the shit of capital', in 'Libidinal Economy' (Lyotard, Jean-François (1993). *Libidinal Economy,* trans. Iain Hamilton Grant. USA: Indiana University Press), he continues, 'in this way you situate yourselves on the most despicable side, the moralistic side where you desire that our capitalized's desire be totally ignored, brought to a standstill, you are like priests with sinners, our servile intensities frighten you, you have to tell yourselves: how they must suffer to endure that! And of course we suffer, we the capitalized, but this does not mean that we do not enjoy...'

The doped-out enjoyment of 'Fendi stores' and manic intensities the speaker portrays is implicated within a growing sense of thematic melancholia, not only within 'Mallwhore Freeestyle', but more broadly across the albums Bladee has come to release. That being said, the speaker also divulges a moralistic underpinning, here: 'Black gloves on, yeah, I'm lookin' hardcore / Hitman, yeah, I'm rockin' with the dark lord...' There is no sanctimony to the lyrics, in fact, the ontological structure of the consumer experience is rendered exactly as is; darker than light – shaded.

In terms of an analysis of Lyotard, however, I recall, once again, Fisher's 'Post Capitalist Desire'. If we are operating exclusively inside the workings of a capitalist (hyper)realism within a track such as 'Mallwhore Freeestyle', then, as Fisher suggest of Lyotard, do we come to 'reject any attempt to find an outside to capitalism[?]' Afterall, '... the proletariat cannot be assigned to a position of the outside.' Perhaps 'Mallwhore Freeestyle' represents exactly this; the post-proletariat voice assigned to the ambient presence of the mall, the Baudrillardian 'shopping centre, the city of the future,

[...] the sublimate of all real life, of all objective social life, in which not only work and money disappear, but also the seasons, those distant vestiges of a cycle which has at last also been homogenized!'

'Mallwhore Freeestyle' acknowledges the fundamental ontological positioning, we are reminded with these lyrics, the digitalised and autotuned messaging also, that before we even start out from any position of analysis, we must register ourselves as being fully homogenized by the system, this is to say, we are always implicated by what we seek to critique. With the sign-values and operative workings of the hyperreal aside, Bladee's assessment is significant: 'Sometimes *I don't understand what it's all for*' he sings, 'But I understand when they see me, then they all sore...' This is the radical proposition offered by the artist, here – within the hyperreal capture of instantaneous answers, the prophet first admits to precisely not knowing.

145   In its current form, the democratic process works as a strategy adopted to make us believe in structural change. It seems the belief in structural change – that a structural change can ever occur – has become the deterrence of change itself. As long as there's an ongoing faith in change – that change might occur within the system, maybe soon, maybe in some far-off, distant future – the system functions. In this way, the sustained faith in democratic, structural changes can be framed as a fatal strategy.

> "I hope that my standpoint isn't wistful or passive." Baudrillard responds to Florian Rötzer, "There's always the objection that I'm so pessimistic, nihilistic or apocalyptic. I don't feel it's optimistic or pessimistic. Rather it's a question of driving logic into an over logic, and then seeing what comes of it. People who always seek to conjure up opposing values or older values are pessimistic; they are the really passive nihilists, as Nietzsche says. The system itself is nihilistic."

I would take this further and say philosophical accelerationism, the desire to accelerate capitalism by way of a terminal velocity, can be reducible to a Baudrillardian fatal strategy.

146   デーモンAstari. (2015). *LiL PEEP - nothing to u (Official Music Video)*. Available: https://www.youtube.com/watch?v=aEnV66QkwNk Last accessed 9th Oct 2020.

147   Yung Lean. (2020). *Yung Lean — Put Me In A Spell (Official Audio)*. Available: https://www.youtube.com/watch?v=KC4SgP1Gqnw Last accessed 9th Oct 2020.
148   Mishima, Y (2001). *The Temple of the Golden Pavilion*, trans. Morris, I. London: Vintage.
149   Lil Peep. (2016). *lil peep x lil tracy - white wine*. Available: https://www.youtube.com/watch?v=wckAAh-V428 Last accessed 9th Oct 2020.
150   *Pirates of the Caribbean: The Curse of the Black Pearl*, 2003, DVD, Walt Disney Pictures, Jerry Bruckheimer Films, US, distributed by Buena Vista Pictures Distribution, directed by Gore Verbinski.
151   *A Cure for Wellness*, 2016, Online Streaming Service (Netflix), Regency Enterprises, Blind Wink Productions, New Regency Productions, US, distributed by 20th Century Fox, directed by Gore Verbinski.
152   'The Temple of the Golden Pavilion, novel by Mishima Yukio, first published in Japanese as Kinkakuji in 1956. The novel is considered one of the author's masterpieces. A fictionalized account of the actual torching of a Kyōto temple by a disturbed Buddhist acolyte in 1950, the novel reflects Mishima's preoccupations with beauty and death.' Encyclopaedia Britannica. (2015). *The Temple of the Golden Pavilion novel by Mishima*. Available: https://www.britannica.com/topic/The-Temple-of-the-Golden-Pavilion Last accessed 9th Oct 2020. 'The great dualities of Nietzsche's philosophy: the Apollonian verses the Dionysian principle, active verse passive nihilism, as well as such of his leading concepts as 'eternal recurrence' and 'love of fate', remained the guiding principles of Mishima's thought throughout his entire career. […] Mishima's nihilism, his sense of the nothingness of reality and the meaningless of life itself, a sense which continually undermines any small momentary comfort his heroes take in a tentative 'faith' or in melodramatic role-playing. […] This was Mishima's real 'act of courage': not the self-indulgent sword-play with which he mesmerized the world but the devastating honesty with which, in his writing, he unmasked his fictional *alter egos* and revealed the void which gaped behind the mask […] Mishima sometimes referred to himself as a nihilist, and […] Noguchi Takehiko speaks of his 'nihilist aesthetics', by which he seems to mean Mishima's attraction to death and night and blood'.' Starrs,

Roy. (1994). *Deadly Dialectics: Sex, Violence, and Nihilism in the World of Yukio Mishima.* North America: University of Hawaii Press. 'In Mishima's novels, as in [Thomas] Mann's, there is a continual, obsessive return to the themes of sickness, deformity, crime and decadence as obvious symptoms and symbols of the nihilism which pervades modern society. But Mishima goes one step further: he does not merely describe nihilism, he embraces it. In this he parts company with Mann – and ultimately also with Nietzsche. For in Mishima nihilism is not merely a problem of modern society; it is a tendency rooted deeply in his own psyche and in that of his alter egos, the protagonists of his novels. Mishima's nihilism begins on the level of instinct and only later is it articulated into a rationally ordered philosophy. In other words, Mishima did not suddenly become a nihilist when, as a teenager, he first read Nietzsche, and thereupon artificially transplant Nietzsche's philosophy into his own writings. One thing that his autobiographical novel, *Confessions of a Mask*, makes clear is that, if he was not quite born a nihilist, he at least acquired nihilistic tendencies, what he called "my heart's leaning toward Death and Night and Blood", at a very early age.' Starrs, Roy. (1991). *Nietzschean Dialectics in the Novels of Mishima Yukio.* Available: https://www.oag.uni-hamburg.de/noag/noag-149-150-1991/noag-1991-3.pdf Last accessed 14th Oct 2020.

153 Lil Peep. (2020). *Lil Peep - OMFG (Official Audio).* Available:https://www.youtube.com/watch?v=KI1Qpuv_z_U Last accessed 14th Oct 2020.

154 HD LYRIC VIDEOS. (2017). *Lil Peep - Lie To Me (Lyrics).* Available: https://www.youtube.com/watch?v=7UGEL_CiRQQ Last accessed 14th Oct 2020.

155 drain gang. (2018). *bladee - That Thing You Do (ft. Uli K).* Available: https://www.youtube.com/watch?v=Mo8VpWSfOU0 Last accessed 14th Oct 2020.

156 drain gang. (2018). *bladee - Nike Just Do It (เกาะเสม็ด).* Available: https://www.youtube.com/watch?v=7WQDckhcF9k Last accessed 14th Oct 2020.

157 Jazzy Jones. (2016). *Miles Davis - Sketches of Spain (1960) (Full Album).* Available: https://www.youtube.com/watch?v=mSS5p9BdNGU Last accessed 14th Oct 2020.

158 Orchidonfire. (2008). *Orchid - I am Nietzche.* Available: https://www.youtube.com/watch?v=edpot4xOqsI Last

accessed 14th Oct 2020.
159   Gorglazon. (2008). *Pg.99 - In Love With An Apparition.* Available: https://www.youtube.com/watch?v=mahS6DCwy_U Last accessed 14th Oct 2020.
160   crazypluto. (2008). *Circle Takes The Square - Non-Objective Portrait of Karma.* Available: https://www.youtube.com/watch?v=_SqYoJhs7Tk Last accessed 14th Oct 2020.
161   I Hate Myself - Topic. (2018). *Caught in a Flood With the Captain of the Cheerleading Squad.* Available: https://www.youtube.com/watch?v=Ro9NzQ15254 Last accessed 14th Oct 2020.
162   Nicolás. (2014). *Saetia - A Retrospective (Full Album).* Available: https://www.youtube.com/watch?v=q801yAFdBPA Last accessed 14th Oct 2020.
163   Polyvinyl Records. (2019). *American Football - American Football (LP1) [FULL ALBUM STREAM].* Available: https://www.youtube.com/watch?v=QZNYVt87y60 Last accessed 14th Oct 2020.
164   Radiohead. (2016). *OK Computer (Full Album HQ).* Available: https://www.youtube.com/watch?v=jNY_wLukVW0&list=PLxzSZG7g8c8x6GYz_FcNr-3zPQ7npP6WF Last accessed 14th Oct 2020.
165   Radiohead. (2016). *Climbing Up the Walls.* Available: https://www.youtube.com/watch?v=XX4EpkR-Sp4 Last accessed 14th Oct 2020.
166   MYSTIC PIMP. (2016). *Lil Peep - Falling 4 Me.* Available: https://www.youtube.com/watch?v=vliInH1gOwc Last accessed 14th Oct 2020.
167   Radiohead. (2015). *Radiohead - Karma Police.* Available: https://www.youtube.com/watch?v=1uYWYWPc9HU Last accessed 14th Oct 2020.
168   The following essay was originally published at the 'International Academic Journal Baudrillard Now'. (Mazey, Alexzander. (2020). A Matrix of Melancholia: Mark Fisher and Jean Baudrillard. *International Academic Journal Baudrillard Now.* Volume 1, Issue 2 (7), p63 - 73.)

> 'Cinema is the art of appearances, tells us something about reality itself. It tells us something about how reality constitutes itself. There is an old gnostic theory that our world was not perfectly created. That the God who created our world was an idiot who bangled the job

so that our world is a half-finished creation. There are voids, openings, gaps, it's not fully real, fully constituted. In the wonderful scene, in the last instalment of the Alien Saga, 'Alien Resurrection' (1997), when Ripley, the cloned Ripley, enters a mysterious room, she encounters the previous, failed version of herself […] Just a horrified creature, a small foetus-like entity, then more developed forms. Finally, a creature that almost looks like her, but her limbs are like that of the monster. This means that all the time, our previous, ultimate embodiments, what we might have been, but are not, that this ultimate versions of ourselves are haunting us. That's the ontological view of reality, that we get here. As if it's an unfinished universe. This is, I think, a very modern feeling, it is true, such ontology of unfinished reality, that cinema became a truly modern art.'

Slavoj Žižek, 'The Pervert's Guide to Cinema'. (Fiennes, Sophie, Slavoj Žižek, Martin Rosenbaum, Georg Misch, Ralph Wieser, Remko Schnorr, Ethel Shepherd, and Tony Myers. (2006) *The Pervert's Guide to Cinema*. London: P Guide.)

What's so frustrating about the characters Jason Statham tends to portray, is their melancholic disposition, the subservience and passive acceptance to an order of appearances that seems to drive humanity towards its own destruction. There is a perverse maturity to this cynicism, however, a sadness that asks what a single man can do against such reckless hatred? Even so, at no point does Jonas Taylor, the protagonist of 'The Meg' (2018, Online Streaming Service (SkyGo), Gravity Pictures, Flagship Entertainment, Apelles Entertainment, Di Bonaventura Pictures, Maeday Productions, US/China, distributed by Warner Bros., directed by Jon Turteltaub), for example, question the ontological nature of the world he has just saved – the metastatic world of decadence and ecstatic communication, finding representation in Sanya Bay, for instance. (Who is he to judge, after all?) In this way, Jonas Taylor, in particular, represents a philosophy of preservation without question; in other words, a philosophy of simple obedience.

What's more frustrating is a trilogy of films like 'The Matrix Saga', particularly the final film of that trilogy, 'The Matrix Revolutions' (2003, DVD, Village Roadshow Pictures, NPV Entertainment, Silver Pictures, US, distributed by Warner

— Sad Boy Aesthetics —

Bros., directed by the Wachowskis) in which the character, Morpheus (Laurence Fishburne), full of a paradoxical faith in his reality inside Zion, looks to the sky and says, 'I imagined this moment, for so long.' Tears form in his eyes. 'Is this real?' He asks.

Compare, briefly, the expressions of the two characters within that brilliant scene. Niobe (Jada Pinkett Smith) stands, looking up at the retreating army of sentinel machines, a face characterised by pure alleviation and relief. She turns, drastically, to face Morpheus, (her own 'referential' of hope and optimistic faith (her love, no less)), who has retreated now, not towards another human being, but into the introspection of himself. Niobe embraces Morpheus, holding him tightly, grounding herself (and him?) into something real, that is to say, into the referential of *faith.* Meanwhile, Morpheus closes his eyes, blinds himself, so to speak, to the knowledge that this just *doesn't feel real – something is off.* 'I imagined this moment, for so long. Is this real?' The very formulation of this question, in the hour of victory, no less, seems revealing.

This is where the film should have begun, I claim; with a character being given the world in which they *imagined*, that is to say, a world they always desired, only to see them begin to question the manifestation of that very same world, as yet another potential simulation – a simulation they did not see coming. The fact that Niobe continues to embrace Morpheus, whilst Morpheus, on the other hand, tentatively looks away from her, back up towards the sky, is interesting. Moreover, it is coincidental, perhaps, how the scene cuts away to an establishing shot of the machine city, followed by a close-up of a *blinded* Neo (Keanu Reeves); a bandage wrapped around his eyes. The *simulated nature* of this secondary world, (the world occurring outside of the *known simulation* of the matrix), can be located, I think, in the strange, melodramatic, (almost silly) representation of the 'machine city' itself, which seems both *weird and eerie.* (I am recalling to mind, for instance, the 'machine face' that converses with Neo, towards the end of the trilogy.)

It is important to compare these twisted, grotesque machines, those who occupy the machine city, whom possess, in addition, a demonic-like quality in appearance, to their 'programmed' counterparts, the machine-minds, full of sentience and occasionally warm wisdom, that appear frequently in the illusory world of the Matrix. Take, for example, the conversation between Neo and Rama Kandra in 'The Matrix Revolutions'. Rama Kandra, we are told, is the machine 'program', the power plant systems' manager for recycling operations.

Nevertheless, Rama appears warm and human; more human than human, perhaps? In fact, Rama is a thoroughly hyperreal mimicry of the human manifestation. 'I love my daughter very much...' He tells, Neo, 'I find her to be the most beautiful thing I have ever seen.' Neo is confused, here; how can a computer program understand something as complex as love. It is a human emotion, after all. 'No, it is a word.' Rama replies. 'What matters is the connection the word implies.'

In the essay, 'The Slow Cancellation of the Future', published in 'Ghosts of my Life', Mark Fisher writes how, '...any particular linguistic term gains its meaning not from its own positive qualities but from its difference from other terms.' It can be said that these linguistic differences exist within a complex, virtual, spectral 'cyberspace' that recalls the absence of additional linguistic terms. These terms exist as a referential spectre. Fisher concludes: '... think of hauntology as *the agency of the virtual*, with the spectre understood not as anything supernatural, but as that which acts without (physically) existing.' Alternatively, in 'Fatal Strategies', Jean Baudrillard writes, 'Signs don't draw up a contract of exchange with each other, *but a pact of alliance.*' (Emphasis added.)

If the cohabitation of Neo and Rama, in a world reserved for the passing of computer programs, does not confirm Neo as yet another computer program, destined (programmed) to eradicate the violent, metastatic ghosts of the matrix, (finding representation in exiled program, Smith (Hugo Weaving), for example), then I don't know what will. In fact, was the love between Rama and his daughter, in addition, programmed into them, more importantly, was the love between Neo and Trinity (Carrie-Anne Moss) also programmed? If so, does this programming, the sentience felt by all involved, *make it any less real?*

'What is real?' Morpheus asks Neo. 'How do you define real? If you're talking about what you can feel, what you can smell, taste and see then real is simply electrical signals interpreted by your brain.'

We know, in addition, from his conversations with the oracle and the architect of the matrix, for example, that Neo has faced a journey of *Eternal Reoccurrence*. Is this not the fate of a program carrying out its protocols, coming to fruition, before repeating again and again, cycling endlessly? In addition, can we not view the faith exhibited by Morpheus, especially towards the destiny of Neo, as something programmed into him? In this way, can we not view faith, in an ontological outlook, for instance, as *a programmable paradigm?*

Moreover, this conversation, between Rama and Neo, takes place within a train station, a subway terminal, a visual presentation of a 'nowhere' place, a (hyperreal) place that exists between both the world of the matrix, and the 'elsewhere' world where programs are created. (Interestingly enough, we never come to observe this world, or its functions.)

It is no matter of convenience that so much of late capitalism's 'non-places' feature heavily in the mise en scène of *'The Matrix Trilogy'*. Consider, for example, the prevalence of these places, the frequent inclusion of elevators, subways, terminal stations, hotel lobbies... In fact, the entire environment of the Matrix, with all its illusory artifice, seems to be defined by the presence of a cultural expectation, the expectation, whilst saturated with the iconography of billboards and advertisement, of progressive modernity as something constantly in a state of progression – although thoroughly unhappy with itself, never settled; pushing forward to someplace, somewhere, endlessly.

The environment, as such, becomes *the simulation of movement, progress, and communication.* The consequence of this environment, a simulated progression towards increasingly compartmentalised (abstract) worlds of work and leisure, (perhaps?) as Fisher points out, develops into, with severe consequences, a culture that has 'lost the ability to grasp and articulate the present.' As Fisher recalls, '...in one very important sense, there is no present to grasp and articulate any more.' In fact, within 'The Slow Cancellation of the Future', Mark Fisher explores the *simulations* inherent in contemporary culture. Culture, (music, especially), occurring at the turn of the century, that is to say, a culture built as the simulacrum of the past. Mark Ronson's simulation of the '60s soul sound', for example, or alternatively, as Fisher writes,

Artic Monkeys' 'discrepancies in texture' placing them; 'neither to the present nor to the past but to some implied 'timeless' era, an eternal 1960s or an eternal 80s.'

It is wrong for Fisher to see these manifestations as a mere 'cancellation of the future' as, I claim, we should observe them, instead, as *cancellations of the past*; the attempts of a abstractive, vibrationally present 'non-place', built on the trajectory of neoliberal (hyper)capitalism, to assimilate and eradicate the 'stagnant communication' of some concrete past; with all its nuance, complexity, and perspective. This is the eradication and assimilation of the past, particularly, as a nostalgic birthing point of *the lost referential* – points of moral and ethical absolutism that are increasingly lost to us, optimistically speaking, assimilated into the relativism of the present. There is an attempt, through the cultural milieu, especially, to rewrite the past into another simulated, proliferated, replicated, 'non-place', a past captured through mediated forms – not for some peripheral, nostalgic purposes – but for the eradication (assimilation) of *what no longer belongs here*. After all, the only referential that should belong here, are those referentials built on the foundations of postmodern relativity, in other words, the relativity of the simulation itself. In this way, the future develops as a simulation in which the past has been thoroughly rewritten.

According to the ideals of progress – the kind that controls, with an everyday influence, thoughts and behaviour – the 'evil past', operating as a 'referential' to the 'brilliant future', is almost always presented as a place of gloom, doom and backwardness. (A backwardness, existing as a 'tenacious myth', that must be thoroughly overcome.) These days, the past becomes the simulation of a non-place, where women died in childbirth, children died without a bite to eat, and suffering and oppression were common place. Paradoxically speaking, this alleged world of horror and suffering simultaneously gave birth to a paradigm in which human beings also came to dominate all life on planet earth, filling the world with the ecstatic communication of fridge magnets and fast cars. *Is this real?* I will recall to your mind, Pentti Linkola's 'Can Life Prevail?'

'We can now thank prosperity for bringing us – among other things – two million cars, millions of glowing, electronic entertainment boxes, and many unneeded buildings to cover the green earth. Surplus wealth has led to gambling in the marketplace and rampant social injustice, whereby 'the common people' end up contributing to the construction of golf courses, five-star hotels, and holiday resorts, while fattening Swiss bank accounts. Besides, the people of wealthy countries are the most frustrated, unemployed, unhappy, suicidal, sedentary, worthless and aimless people in history.' (Linkola, Pentti. (2009). *Can Life Prevail?* trans. Corrupt, Inc. UK: Arktos.)

It is fascinating how Mark Fisher writes of an eternal 1960s or an eternal 80s, when we consider, in 'The Matrix' (1999), for example, (the final, cinematic masterpiece of the twentieth century, perhaps?), a humanity that forever resides in an eternal simulation of the 1990s. Take, for instance, the address between Agent Smith and a captured, tortured Morpheus, as we head towards the climax of the earliest instalment of the franchise.

'Have you ever stood and stared at it, marvelled at its beauty, its genius? Billions of people just living out their lives. Oblivious. Did you know that the first matrix was designed to be the perfect human world, where none suffered, where everyone would be happy? It was a disaster, no one would accept the program... Some believed that we lacked the programming language to describe your perfect world, but I believe, as a species, human beings define their reality through misery and suffering. A perfect world was a dream that your primitive cerebrum kept trying to wake up from. Which is why the matrix was redesigned to this, the peak of your civilisation. I say your civilisation because as soon as we started thinking for you it really became our civilisation, which is, of course, what this is all about. Evolution, Morpheus. Evolution, like the dinosaur. Look out that window, you had your time, the future is our world. Morpheus, the future is our time.'

Is Agent Smith referring to the marvelled beauty, the genius of human civilisation, or rather to the machine matrix itself, a world where billions of people live out their lives, and so on, oblivious to the simulation? Interestingly enough, either side of this interpretation holds weight, since both the matrix and the 'peak of human civilisation' can be interpreted as totally illusory constructs, products of marvellous artifice, built on the foundations of a virtual trajectory. What's so fascinating about these allegedly sentient machines, finding representation in Smith, is the inability to break away from the 'referential' nature of modern humanity, finding fruition in the Agent's outlook on progress and evolution. A progressive future, a trajectory towards a utopianism, that has, perhaps, been lost, in addition, to the machine mind, after all, this is a machine sentience, an artificial intelligence, built in the image of human sentience.

It is interesting how Agent Smith, a reflection of the black-suited, 'hard-power' corporatism of the 1990s, is obsessed with both the progress and evolution of his own machine civilisation, and yet comes to develop an incompatibility. He develops, gradually, overtime, into a virus that must be thoroughly eradicated from the same system (trajectory) he once served. (His eradication occurs at the hands of another program, Neo.) Only through the eradication of Smith's belief in progress, (whatever that may look like for an artificial intelligence's perspective), can harmony between the machine consciousness and human existence finally be achieved, in other words, there is a maintenance of an *equilibrium,* here. In another scene, once again, addressing the captured, tortured Morpheus, Agent Smith asks:

'Can you hear me, Morpheus? I'm going to be honest with you. I hate this place, this zoo, this prison, this reality, whatever you want to call it, I can't stand it any longer. It's the smell – if there is such a thing. I feel saturated by it. I can taste your stink; and every time I do, I fear that I have somehow been infected by it. It's repulsive. Isn't it? I must get out of here. I must get free, and this mind is the key. My key. Once Zion is destroyed there is no need for me to be here. Do you understand? ...I need to get inside Zion.'

In terms of Agent Smith, the philosophy of progress exists in tandem with *resentment and misanthropy.* This reveals, I claim, the nature of progressive values as concealing a hatred for the existence of the present, which must be constantly worked upon, a philosophy where society will always perceive the iconography of the present as the iconography of its own 'backwardness', a *stink* that must be thoroughly eradicated. Ergo, progress develops as a philosophy of self-loathing and resentment. This is why our progressive societies must always occupy a virtual future, a virtual trajectory, whereby the present must be dominated by the iconography, the sign-values, so to speak, of human progress (technological and economic, for example). (The ideologies of progress are something we continuously observe in the ecstatic communication of consumer culture, for example, with each newly-released, upgraded, worked-upon commodity.) The future is only ever a day away; whilst the present, on the other hand, is designed to remind us of the future, with the present's incessant replaying of the past, that is to say, *a simulated past* as an operative 'referential' for *a simulated future.* Stagnancy, particularly in regards to things like economics and social justice, in this case, becomes a referential evil, a threat to survival, that must be thoroughly overcome.

When you really think about it, achievements, particularly in terms of social justice, for example, have not really occurred from the mindset of relativity and progress, but rather from a paradigm of pure absolutism, the absolutist philosophy, for instance, of a principled, human equality. (Absolutism in *The Golden Rule,* for instance.) These achievements were born, not of progress, or social democracy, but perhaps from a collective consciousness that always existed, manifesting, perhaps, in the earliest religions of the world, albeit *lost* in the atomisation of the self. This lost, collective ontology worked towards an equilibrium with the cosmic order, perhaps, whilst simultaneously seeking the eradication of exploitative, fascistic materialism. This materialism continuously seeking the atomised – relative – alleviation of suffering, particularly at the expense of other agents in the world; exploited agents who are, more often than not, viewed as thoroughly lesser beings. This was the case with slave ownership, for example. One contention persists in how the abolition of slavery only occurred when slaves became more beneficial as agents in a progressive trajectory geared, increasingly, towards commodity consumption. In other words, agents were freed (assimilated) into a mode of being in the world that thoroughly diffused a revolutionary potential.

Either way, the victories of emancipation have been thoroughly absorbed into the mythology of progress. In addition, the nature of suffering, particularly as a 'referential evil', goes hand in hand with both the trajectory of progress, and the trajectories of religion. Every day, these trajectories appear, increasingly, like the beliefs of a religious cult, built on the foundations of a mythological past. The melancholia that defines the twenty-first century emanates from this cult's inability to materialise a satisfying destination, a *lost* absolutism, a *lost* referential, so to speak, since the trajectory of civilisation must always remain virtual, always hyperreal. It is easy to imagine our current trajectory's path, as a path of mass extinction, no less, when you consider those religious cults, failing to manifest a tangible destination for its followers, resulting in mass suicide. Death is the only plausible destination, here.

In many ways, the 1990s was a thoroughly unsatisfying destination since it was built on an illusory faith. A faith driven by the idea that suffering, standing as a 'referential evil', was not something to be integrated into daily existence, but rather something to be thoroughly eradicated, marginalised, ignored. These days, the utopian ideals of progress, preached by progressives the world over, have developed towards a virtual trajectory that exists, allegedly, on the right side of history. Ironically, the right side of history will actually occupy a world in which the cults of progress, full of cancerous metastasis, will be thoroughly eradicated. After all, survival must be defined by an equilibrium, not progress.

It is ironic that Agent Smith, towards the end of the trilogy, manifests into a reflection of 'the virus' he observes in humanity. In fact, the matrix seems like an ideal way for the machine world to encapsulate the paradoxical, rational 'human' hatred for existence, in the form of a program (Agent Smith), that can become eradicated by the irrational 'human' love for existence, taking shape in another program, (Neo). The matrix becomes a world where human sentience, alongside the human residue of a machine consciousness, (both full of paradox), can endlessly reoccur. In this way, the matrix develops as *a program of regulation*. It is not difficult to imagine this machine sentience as a sentience infused with human incompatibilities and paradox, incompatibilities that must be regulated to an elsewhere world; a simulacrum. Even so, the machine world believes itself to be morally superior to humanity, since it can live in accordance to a harmonious *equilibrium* – an equilibrium achieved through the interplay of compartmentalised worlds. Once again, talking to Morpheus, Agent Smith shares a revelation:

> 'I'd like to share a revelation I've had, during my

– Sad Boy Aesthetics –

> time here. It came to me when I tried to classify your species. I realised that you're not actually mammals. Every mammal, on this planet, instinctively develops a natural equilibrium with the surrounding environment but you humans do not. You move to an area and you multiply and multiply until every natural resource is consumed and the only way you can survive is to spread to another area. There is another organism on this planet that follows the same pattern, do you know what it is? A virus. Human beings are a disease. A cancer of this planet. You are a plague, and we are the cure.'

Firstly, it is implied, through Smith's revelation, that humanity is best defined as a thoroughly lesser species, as a virus; this is self-evident in the pontification, here. Through this analysis, however, Smith also implies something of the machine world itself. According to Smith, this must be a world occupying a paradigm of equilibrium. In this way, the artificial intelligence – the machine world – developed as a 'cure' to humanities imbalance, AI is seen, by Smith, at least, as an evolutionary progression, an improvement on humanities' recklessness. It is fascinating how an artificial intelligence, a program, like Agent Smith, for example, can come to this personal revelation, almost as if this revelation was, in some way, a programmed manifestation, an inevitability that came to fruition during his time in the matrix – 'I'd like to share a revelation I've had, *during my time here.*' Through his exposure to 'the stink' of humanity, there develops, inside Agent Smith, a hatred for humanity; a hatred so powerful that Smith, in fact, becomes the virus he despises, existing, eventually, outside of the delicate equilibrium of the matrix. In Smith's desire for the eradication of a liberated humanity, (a liberation finding representation in the existence of Zion), Smith's own existence, that is to say, his being in the world, can finally come to an end – 'I can taste your stink; and every time I do, I fear that I have somehow been infected by it.' Moreover, it is implied, throughout the trilogy, that Smith's existence is insufferable to him – 'I must get free, and this mind is the key. My key. Once Zion is destroyed there is no need for me to be here. Do you understand?'

Secondly, similar to Neo's conceptions of love, as a human emotion, can we not view this hatred in a similar way? It seems the matrix becomes the model, the means, in which the machines themselves are able to function, within these processes of eternal reoccurrence, that is to say, within an equilibrium. It is fascinating how both the human emotions of love and hate manifest in the artificial consciousnesses, the programs, that come to define the machine world. I claim the human element, the *residue* of the human condition, especially within the machine consciousness, (built in the image of human sentience, remember?), is regulated by the matrix itself, which is why the existence of the matrix was far more than a means of power relay, in fact – the matrix was absolutely necessary to the machine's own survival in terms of a regulatory system of the machine's human residue. Morpheus states that the matrix was the source of the machine city's power, a means of harvesting naturally-occurring human energy, in this way, however, I claim the matrix was actually the source of the machine world's equilibrium. It became the means in which the human and the machine could coexist. 'I love my daughter very much…' Rama tells Neo, 'I find her to be the most beautiful thing I have ever seen.' Rama's daughter, Sati, is a collective representation of the human element, of course, a consciousness sent to the matrix, by Rama, a machine program, as a means of protection.

> "Are you from the Matrix?" Sati asks Neo.
> "Yes, no." Neo replies. "I mean, I was."
> …
> "Sati, come here, darling." Rama calls from the subway platform. "Leave the poor man in peace."
> "Yes, Papa."
> "I am sorry, *she is still very curious.*"

Does it seem unusual for the machine mind, the AI consciousness, to both love and despise its human creator? This is, after all, the same human creator, full of curiosity, that gave birth to a sentient, intelligent race of machines. It seems the matrix becomes a world where the human conceptions of love and hate formulate, in the minds of programs, at least, only to become eradicated by one another, before the cycle repeats, endlessly, through Eternal Reoccurrence. In other words, the reoccurrence develops as the equilibrium itself. I will recall to your mind an opening scene of the trilogy, where Morpheus explains the origins of the matrix.

> 'This is the world that you know. The world as it was

at the end of the twentieth century. It exists now only as a neuro-interactive simulation that we call the matrix. You've been living in a dream world, Neo. This is the world as it exists today. Welcome to the desert of the real. We have only bits and pieces of information but what we know for certain is that at some point in the early twenty-first century, all of mankind was united in celebration. We marvelled in our own magnificence as we gave birth to AI [Artificial Intelligence]. A singular consciousness that spawned an entire race of machines. We don't know who struck first – us or them – but we know that it was us that scorched the sky. At the time, they were dependant on solar power, and it was believed that they would be unable to survive without an energy source as abundant as the sun. Throughout human history, we have been dependant on machines to survive. Fate, it seems, is not without a sense of irony.'

Several points of contention arise with Morpheus' explanation, here. Firstly, how does Morpheus know this is not a secondary dream world, a secondary neuro-interactive simulation, a simulation of the desert of the real, which appears, less like a desert, and more like a potent landscape, complete with thunder, lightning, and the ruins of a twenty-first century civilisation? In terms of Baudrillardian analysis, this is where problems within the matrix trilogy arise – not as a good representation of the hyperreal, but rather as a misreading, since Baudrillard's 'desert of the real' is thoroughly indistinguishable from *true reality*. Why? Because true reality does not really exist, since, once again, 'the simulacrum is never what hides the truth – it is the truth that hides the fact that there is none.' Ironically, I believe Jean Baudrillard's problem with *'The Matrix'* arises from this reading of a misreading. (After all, The Matrix is a poor representation of the Borges fable, whereby the map of the empire, and the empire itself, becomes thoroughly indistinguishable.) Within the Matrix, there is a clear difference between the matrix, and the allegedly true reality that Morpheus occupies; in other words, there is an apparent distinguishability. The operative word here is *apparent*, since the world Morpheus occupies seems, in addition, thoroughly illusory. It is perhaps another dream world, another neuro-interactive simulation, only questioned when Morpheus is given the world he envisioned.

"I imagined this moment, for so long. Is this real?" Ironically speaking, Morpheus *has* defined his reality – up until this point – through misery and suffering. These conceptions of misery and suffering have been sustained by a tertiary subject; that is of Morpheus' *faith*. A faith in the fateful trajectory of 'The One' to deliver a liberation from the machine construct. Our own misery and suffering are defined, I claim, by a similar faith. A faith in the fateful trajectory of progress as leading towards the alleviation of both our misery and suffering.

Peripherally speaking, a secondary point of evidence for this theory arises with Morpheus' explanation of this race of machines, particularly in regards to their dependence on solar power. This theory seems incompatible with 'The Matrix Revolutions', since we see Neo and Trinity breach the storm clouds, where Trinity sees the sublime brilliance of the sun, for the first time in her life, whispering the word, 'Beautiful', before the ship, like Icarus, plummets back down towards the machine city. We are led to believe that this artificial intelligence, whilst creating a complex matrix world to enslave humanity, were simultaneously unable to create a suitable means of breaching this cloud coverage, accessing 'an energy source as abundant as the sun.' This moment reveals, I claim, the true purpose of the matrix, not merely as a source of power for the machine world, but as the model in which the machine consciousness achieves its own equilibrium. However, for the human subject, of course, this equilibrium seems thoroughly undesirable. In 'Fatal Strategies', Baudrillard writes:

> 'Each of us secretly prefers an arbitrary and cruel order, one that leaves us no choice, to the horrors of a liberal one where we don't even know what we want, where we are forced to recognize that we don't know what we want; for in the former case we are consigned to maximal determination, and in the second to indifference. Everyone secretly prefers an order so rigorous, as unfolding of events so arbitrary (or so illogical, as with fate or ceremony) that the slightest disturbance can make the whole thing collapse – everyone prefers this to the dialectical workings of reason, where a finalizing logic dominates all accidents of language.'

> *'Fate, it seems, is not without a sense of irony.'*

Even so, progress, in this way, becomes a utopian vision

that will never materialise, but instead continue recklessly towards a trajectory of a utopian faith that, in addition, conceals the utopia's very absence, particularly as a state of equilibrium. (The equilibrium necessary for human survival.) In Baudrillard's thinking, this was, technically speaking, the utopia of modernism that had already been realised in the late twentieth century, yet seemed, in hindsight, deeply inadequate, as this world, paradoxically speaking, could not exist without a sense of continuous, virtual trajectory. (The trajectory of a metastatic economic growth, for instance.)

In the essay, 'On Nihilism', appearing in 'Simulacra and Simulation', Baudrillard writes, 'There are cultures that have no imaginary except of their origin and have no imaginary of their end. There are those that are obsessed by both...', he concludes, 'It is this melancholia that is becoming our fundamental passion.'

Fisher, on the other hand, locates the *melancholic* hauntology, defined in 'The Slow Cancellation of the Future', as perhaps, the result of 'neoliberal capitalism's destruction of solidarity and security', a destruction (eradication) that 'brought about a compensatory hungering for the well-established and the familiar[.]' In other words, the virtual trajectory of neoliberal capitalism, infected by hauntological awareness, became haunted by an absolutism, that is to say, a lost referential that we can now only recall through *simulated nostalgia*. Compare, briefly, Fisher's conclusion with Baudrillard's statement in 'On Nihilism', 'Melancholia is the inherent quality of the mode of disappearance of meaning, of the mode of the volatilization of meaning in operational systems. And we are all melancholic.'

In the introduction to Baudrillard's 'Fatal Strategies', Dominic Pettman, writes:

> 'To come of age in the late 1980s and early 1990s was to find oneself in a sociopolitical echo chamber, robbed even of the false promise of revolution, or compensatory hope of utopia... The temptation is to simplify the insights... just as the Wachowski brothers did in their naïve homage to the great man, *The Matrix* (As Baudrillard eventually pointed out, *The Matrix* is the kind of film the Matrix itself would have made about the Matrix.) Rescuing Baudrillard's ideas from caricature thus becomes a challenging and important task, now that he is no longer

– Alex Mazey –

with us.'

Without the 'progressive' trajectory of the future, without the 'backwardness' of the past, the present would articulate our preferable catastrophe as a simulacrum of an imaginary absolutism; a hyperreal absolutism that whilst never actually found, would *feel*, at times, entirely lost.

169   *2001: A Space Odyssey*, 1968, DVD, Stanley Kubrick Productions, UK, distributed by Metro-Goldwyn-Mayer, directed by Stanley Kubrick.

170   *The Shining*, 1980, DVD, The Producer Circle Company, Peregrine Productions, Hawk Films, US, distributed by Warner Bros., directed by Stanley Kubrick.

171   Fisher, Mark. (2019). *Kubrick as Cold Rationalist*. Available: https://www.reddit.com/r/StanleyKubrick/comments/9uuuqw/mark_fisher_on_kubrick_what_is_unmistakably_still/ Last accessed 14th Oct 2020.

172   *Eyes Wide Shut*, 1999, Online Streaming Service (Netflix), Stanley Kubrick Productions, Pole Star, Hobby Films, US, distributed by Warner Bros., directed by Stanley Kubrick.

173   *Metropolis*, 2001, DVD, Madhouse, Japan, distributed by Toho, directed by Rintaro.

174   *Dune*, 1984, DVD, Dino De Laurentiis Corporation, US, distributed by Universal Pictures, directed by David Lynch.

175   *Midsommar*, 2019, Online Streaming Service (Amazon Prime), Square Peg, B-Reel Films, US, distributed by A24 (United States), Nordisk Film (Sweden), directed by Ari Aster.

176   *Hereditary*, 2018, Online Streaming Service (Netflix), A24, PalmStar Media, Finch Entertainment, Windy Hill Pictures, US, distributed by A24, directed by Ari Aster.

177   Never forget the (habitual) laws of this universe that remain undiscovered.

178   Belle Delphine: E-girl and internet personality known for the commodification of her own bathwater.

179   Wittgenstein, Ludwig. (1973). *Philosophical Investigations,* trans. G.E.M. Anscombe. US: Wiley–Blackwell.

LAY OUT YOUR UNREST

Lightning Source UK Ltd.
Milton Keynes UK
UKHW022037020721
386538UK00007B/444